Pioneer Picnics

Settlers of the East San Gabriel Valley

by Layne D. Staral

Pioneer Picnics, Settlers of the East San Gabriel Valley

ISBN: 979-8-9872836-4-6

All uncredited photos are from the Layne Staral Collection. Both the Azusa and Glendora Historical Museums gave permission for the use of some photos before the date of the printing of each article in the magazine. Those photos and others are credited at the end of the book.

The Memoirs of Frances De Shields Metzger, 1977, Layne Staral Collection.

"The Real Folks" by Mary Margaret De Shields, 1925, Layne Staral Collection.

Design & Layout: Anna Lafferty, Lafferty Design Plus

KIERAN PUBLISHING
P.O. Box 3863
Santa Barbara, CA 93130
www.kieranpublishing.com

The names, dates, and incidents in this book are accurate to the best of the author's knowledge.

To the memory of my great-grandmother,
Maggie De Shields, the secretary and soul
of the Settlers of the East San Gabriel Valley

To local historians who research, record,
and celebrate the past

To the future – Avalon, Ivy, and Rex

And in my heart – Bob Keys

Foreword

I first met Layne Staral about twenty years ago when I began volunteering at the Glendora Historical Society Museum. We quickly became friends and learned that we are related by marriage through early pioneer families in this area.

As a retired English teacher, Layne has the skills needed for writing and is especially proficient at researching and writing about early San Gabriel Valley history. This is evidenced by the articles she wrote for the *Glendoran* magazine.

This book is a compilation of those articles. She brings the past to life through her accurate stories and descriptions of the early pioneers of this Valley.

If you are interested in detailed and captivating information of life in the mid-1800s to the early 1900s, especially in the east San Gabriel Valley, this is the book for you!

I believe that the more we understand life as it was in the past, the richer our lives will be!

Enjoy!
Karen Cullen
Descendant of a few pre-Glendora families

Table of Contents

Preface

My brother and I weren't allowed to have friends with us when we went to the pioneer picnics because there wasn't enough room in the car for our small family and the food, too. Besides, we'd have our cousins to play with.

My mother drove us from Eagle Rock east to Azusa City Hall on Colorado and Foothill Boulevards since there was no freeway option in the 1950s and 1960s. The trunk was filled with pioneer haute cuisine: fried chicken, ham with white beans, stuffed bell peppers, hard-boiled eggs in beet juice, homemade butter pickles, potato salad, and pies. My favorite was apple, made by my great-grandmother Maggie De Shields. She was in the car with us and my grandmother. Four generations. And our valley roots went back two more generations to John and Sarah Casey.

Maggie was a big deal at the Settlers of the East San Gabriel Valley picnics, held officially from 1922 to 1973. Even as a child, I knew it. Adults gathered around her, and she got to sit on the stage during their meetings and often spoke. I didn't know which of the elderly settlers bent down to shake my hand when she introduced us, nor did I know she was the one to read the necrology report, the list of settlers who died each year.

She kept track of them all. Secretary of the group for forty-four years, she was the one who sent out postcard invitations and encouraged their families to attend. She had everyone sign the guest book and update their addresses. There were no cell phones or answer phones then, and her notes from each meeting were handwritten in a book. There were several books, lost now, but the last one was found in the Azusa museum not long after I wrote the January 2008 article for the *Glendoran* magazine.

By then, I was volunteering in both the Azusa and Glendora Historical Museums, working on my family history and my articles. The sight of my great-grandmother's handwriting amazed me, and later, I got to hear her voice on one of the reel-to-reel tapes that were sent to the Glendora museum after an elderly member's death. John Lundstrom, then President of the Glendora Historical Society, located funds so I could pay to have the voices transferred from the old tapes to compact discs.

The grandchildren of the original settlers had taped their stories at those picnics. While we children played with young relatives on playground equipment, the old-timers were regaling each other with tales of the Azusa Valley.

Preface

I have a vivid memory of standing — suffering the fatigue of a child who has played too much — beside my mother and brother at the door to the auditorium. My mother had cracked open the door so we could hear what was going on. All I heard was laughter. Belly laughter.

You can hear the joy in the voices on the tapes and compact discs and see it on the faces in the 1927 and 1950 picnic pictures in the Glendora museum. And I am so lucky to have heard that laughter while it was being taped.

The picnics themselves have a history. They were held on Memorial Day every year after a gathering at Fairmount Cemetery. Custodian of the site for years, Lorne Ward's notes were published in the May/Jun 2009 issue of the *Glendoran* and explain the informal start of these gatherings. In the late 1800s, settlers put wooden crosses on a family grave to mark the burial site of a loved one, and the family would care for that piece of land. Over time, the markers deteriorated. Families replaced wooden crosses with stone markers and eventually began meeting to clean the entire graveyard on Memorial Day. Veterans of several wars used the day to honor their dead at a brief service there; then families would have a picnic in a local oak or gum grove.

By the time I was attending picnics, most of them were held at Azusa City Hall because it provided an auditorium where the descendants of the settlers could have their meetings after lunch as well as space to take a long group photograph. The filming of the 1950 photo afforded enough time for the two officers on the left of the group to beat the camera to the right and shake hands.

I enjoyed the research I've done for this book, and I want to share my amazement with you as I have with patient friends who are wonderful listeners. When I started, I didn't know the Caseys, Taggarts, and De Shields were on the pioneer map; I didn't know the Taggart name. When I happened into a real estate office looking for family homes, I was shocked to find a street named Meda. My grandmother called her Aunt Ella. Meda Ella Shepperd was married to George Dexter Whitcomb's son, George Bennett Whitcomb. Since his father was building the town of Glendora and naming streets in 1887, he named one after his daughter-in-law, mother of his first grandson. Today, people wonder who Meda was.

My family talked about the De Shields family citrus groves and the house with a porch that wrapped around it. Gladstone House at 960 E. Gaillard St. is still standing as an historic location with the De Shields name first on the title search report.

I was able to locate Marquita Barber, too, William R. Shepperd's granddaughter who attended school with Mildred "Skeeter" Kobzeff, beloved and longtime historian. Marquita shared her family stories with me, and we identified relatives in old picnic pictures. Her grandfather was Glendora's water dowser. Another surprise.

Of course, I always knew Maggie and Walter De Shields owned and ran the Glendora Market below Glenn Odell's dentistry. My grandmother talks about it a lot in her memoir, written for me in 1977 and included in this book.

The settlers who built the towns in the East San Gabriel Valley didn't work alone. They relied on and married each other, and the women's last names changed. Casey's two daughters' families were Taggarts and De Shields, and while some of my family members later moved to other local towns, most stayed in Glendora as Shepperds, Kamphefners, De Shields, and Whitcombs. These are names on some of the gravestones in Oakdale Cemetery, the memorial park established in the 1890s when Fairmount became too small. I've included a brief family genealogy in the appendix. Even I have to refer to it.

I don't claim to be an historian. I set out to write articles on my family history and found the *Glendoran* magazine and Ida and Joe Fracasse, the latter now gone. Actually, I was introduced to the Fracasses before I had articles in mind, and it was their encouragement that prompted me to start writing. They gave me an outlet for my research. From 2006 to 2011, they published all my family articles, my grandmother's memoirs, and the Cullen and Engelhardt pieces about other families. Their small, independent magazine nurtured a love of history for forty years before shutting down last year. This tenure is an amazing feat for a small publication and bears witness to enthusiastic local history buffs, the power of family lore, and a commitment to harmony and respect.

My endnotes may not be complete. Today, it would be a thankless and infinite job to find the sources I worked with more than ten years ago because museum volunteers often reorganize files and many of my interviewees have died. I'm trusting the research I did for the original articles when I included most attributions in the text itself.

I am also trying to respect spelling choices. My own ancestors spelled Shepperd in numerous ways, and one side of the Engelhardt family is spelled Englehart. I'm struggling to keep the branches straight. Glenn Odell, the town dentist, spelled his name with a double "n," his namesake Glen De Shields with only one.

I have done my best, but any mistakes are mine. I can only hope you enjoy the book despite them.

Layne D. Staral
Monrovia, California
2024

Introduction

To understand local history requires some knowledge of California's past.

This state has always been idyllic. But the mountains, deserts, and ocean bordering the land made it difficult for early settlers to enter it. Native Californians lived isolated here for thousands of years before the Spanish started exploring in the 1540s. Then they ignored the land until 1769 when the first Spanish governor of California founded a settlement in San Diego and so began the mission period of California history. More Spanish governors succeeded him, and during their tenure, the land here belonged mostly to the missions.

Spain ruled Mexico and California until 1822 when Mexico won its battle for independence. After that, Mexican governors of California held office until 1846. Once they had power, they made mission lands secular and used them as rewards, as land grants, for their supporters in both the war with Spain and the Mexican-American War.

My bibliography includes several wonderful books on the history of California. I'm making a valiant attempt to summarize it in two or three paragraphs – an impossible goal – but you have to know that California was inhabited when it became a state in 1850. Too often, an online search for a list of California governors reveals only the U.S. governors from 1849 to the present without acknowledging our Native and Hispanic heritage. It's also helpful to know that land grants and early land purchases involved many disagreements over inaccurate surveys.

Locally, an Englishman on a quest for land got caught in the transition from Mexican to American rule from 1846 to 1849 when U.S. military governors were in control. His name was Henry Dalton. He bought both the Ranchos Azusa and San José, originally Mexican land grants, in 1844.

His land purchases were vast — 45,000 acres of choice land, according to Sheldon G. Jackson, author of *A British Ranchero in Old California: Henry Dalton and the Rancho Azusa*. The Rancho Azusa comprised what is now the town of Azusa and later the San Gabriel and Dalton canyons. His Rancho San José included most of the San Gabriel and Pomona valleys, including what is now Glendora, Claremont, Pomona, La Verne, and San Dimas. To these holdings he added the Rancho Santa Anita which extended west into Pasadena and the Rancho Francisquito, idle mission lands to the west of Rancho Azusa. When asked, Henry Dalton said he owned all the land in all directions from his adobe homestead in the Azusa foothills. He was right. Old maps show how vast his holdings were.

But Dalton's story is a tragedy. He arrived in California determined to buy land, achieved his goal, then spent years in courts trying to prove the boundaries of his holdings and his right to them.

While the United States agreed to honor all Mexican land grants in the Treaty of Guadalupe Hidalgo, ownership was upheld only until fraudulent claims prompted a review of all land holdings. Surveys began. In 1858, a surveyor named Hancock determined that the land between the Azusa and San José ranchos was open and available for homesteading. This land is now Glendora, but there were no towns, no boundaries, no streets then. In 1865, John Casey filed a homestead claim on the 160 acres where Citrus College and Azusa Pacific University are now and set an example for other settlers to do the same. But he didn't receive the deed until 1882 after the court's decision in favor of the settlers and against Dalton. The lawsuits lasted years, long enough for the Casey family to grow and for more settlers to claim homesteads. Dalton was left bankrupt.

The appeal of southern California is legendary. People were promised lands to homestead here. There was the Gold Rush in 1848 that brought venturers west. The Civil War loomed over the eastern United States until 1861 when it started, and many people came west to avoid it. There was a drought in Texas, and undoubtedly threats and natural disasters in other states that pushed people west.

Historians tend to ignore the settlers' stories because they begin at the end of Dalton's tragedy. But the settlers were the ones to build and develop the local towns in the 1880s, and it's their story I want to tell. This book is limited in scope to the temporal gap between 1850 and the early 1900s and to the geographical area included in Dalton's Ranchos Azusa and San José, especially where the towns of Glendora and Azusa are now. The pioneers all knew each other. They took horses and wagons to neighboring homesteads to visit relatives and friends, and enjoyed each other's company. The pioneer picnics were inclusive of all of them.

My subjects are mostly my own ancestors, the Caseys being one set of my great-great-great-grandparents. I'm a sixth generation Californian, and my grandnieces and grandnephew are eighth. So this book is personal and informal. I want to share the lifestyle and minutiae of the founders of this area. Since many of my sources are letters and pictures I've inherited and store in my closets, I've been able to access the minds of my subjects in a way that most historians can't. I am not being scholarly, nor am I bragging. I've accumulated boxes of memorabilia as family members have died. I'm anxious to share their stories with you.

Timeline

c.13,000 to 10,000 BC	Native cultures are established in California.
1542	The Spanish discover and start to explore Alta California.
1771	The San Gabriel Mission is founded.
1776	The Declaration of Independence is written and signed.
1822-1846	Mexico establishes its independence from Spain and starts to govern California.
1844-1846	Henry Dalton, a British merchant, buys the Rancho Azusa, one-third interest in Rancho San José, and its addition for $7,000. Now, the cities of Azusa, San Dimas, and Glendora.
1846	The Mexican-American War starts.
1848	Under the Treaty of Guadalupe Hidalgo, the Mexican-American War ends, and the United States agrees to honor Mexican land grants. The California Gold Rush starts.
1850	California becomes a state.
1852	Dalton files claim to his five ranchos: Azusa; San José Addition (San Dimas, Glendora); one-third of San José (Pomona, Claremont, and La Verne); San Francisquito (Baldwin Park and Irwindale); Santa Anita (Arcadia). They are patented in 1866 and 1867.
1858	Henry Hancock, a government surveyor, claims that the land between Ranchos Azusa and San José is open land, available for homesteading.
1861	The Civil War begins.

1862 A smallpox epidemic occurs in the Azusa Valley.

1865 John Casey files a claim for the 160 acres where Citrus College and Azusa Pacific University are now. The Civil War ends.

1868 Dalton and the settlers build a brush and adobe school.

1870s The citrus industry begins in the valley. In 1874, W.J. De Shields starts planting orange trees with fruit and seeds he purchases in Los Angeles.

1871 The Los Angeles County Board of Supervisors forms the San José Water District.

1872 The Methodist Church South is organized.

1873 The Azusa Township is created.

1881 Dalton attempts to defend his Mexican land grants from homesteaders from 1851 to 1881, but courts rule in favor of the settlers.

1883 Harrison Fuller petitions Washington for a post office that he names Alosta. It is located in the Cullen home in the form of a thread box.

1884 George Dexter Whitcomb visits the Azusa Valley and buys land from Harrison Fuller, W.B. Cullen, James J. West, and Henry D. Engelhardt to start a town that he names Glendora.

Henry Dalton dies in Los Angeles.

1886 The Azusa Land and Water Company lays out Azusa.

1887 Boom. Glendora becomes a town.

Whitcomb surveys and lays out the streets.

Major George E. Gard creates Alosta south of Glendora.

Whitcomb forms the Glendora Land Company and acts as both its president and treasurer.

Whitcomb organizes the Glendora Water Company.

The Glendora Land Company builds Hotel Belleview.

The big land sale is held for lots in the new town.

The Santa Fe Railway is completed through Glendora.

W.B. Cullen makes August Engelhardt a deputy postmaster and moves the post office to his store on the northeast corner of Vista Bonita and Whitcomb Avenues, then the center of town.

The Glendora *Signal* newspaper, published by John Jeffrey, makes its debut.

The Glendora Grammar School opens.

1888 Concern over fires prompts a volunteer fire department to organize in Glendora.

1890 Flora Jones Webb, once owner of the *Glendora Gleaner*, coins the term Pride of the Foothills in the early 1900s.

1893 The A.C.G. Citrus Association is formed by growers in Azusa, Covina, and Glendora. Later, it expands to include more towns and becomes the San Antonio Fruit Exchange.

1895-1920 Public services increase.

1902 Telephone service starts before 1902 in packing houses.

1904 The San Gabriel Valley Gas Company is incorporated in Azusa.

1906 An earthquake levels San Francisco.

1907 On December 20, 1907, Pacific Electric red cars reach Glendora.

1911 Foothill Boulevard is paved, and Glendora is incorporated. Roads are graded and oiled.

1914 World War I begins.

1915 Glendora purchases a fire truck.

1929 The stock market crashes.

1930 The Great Depression starts.

1933 Orton Englehart invents the Rain Bird sprinkler and forms a partnership with marketer Clem La Fetra.

1939 World War II starts.

1945 Japan surrenders.

1955 Disneyland opens.

Original Azusa Valley Homesteaders Map 1937

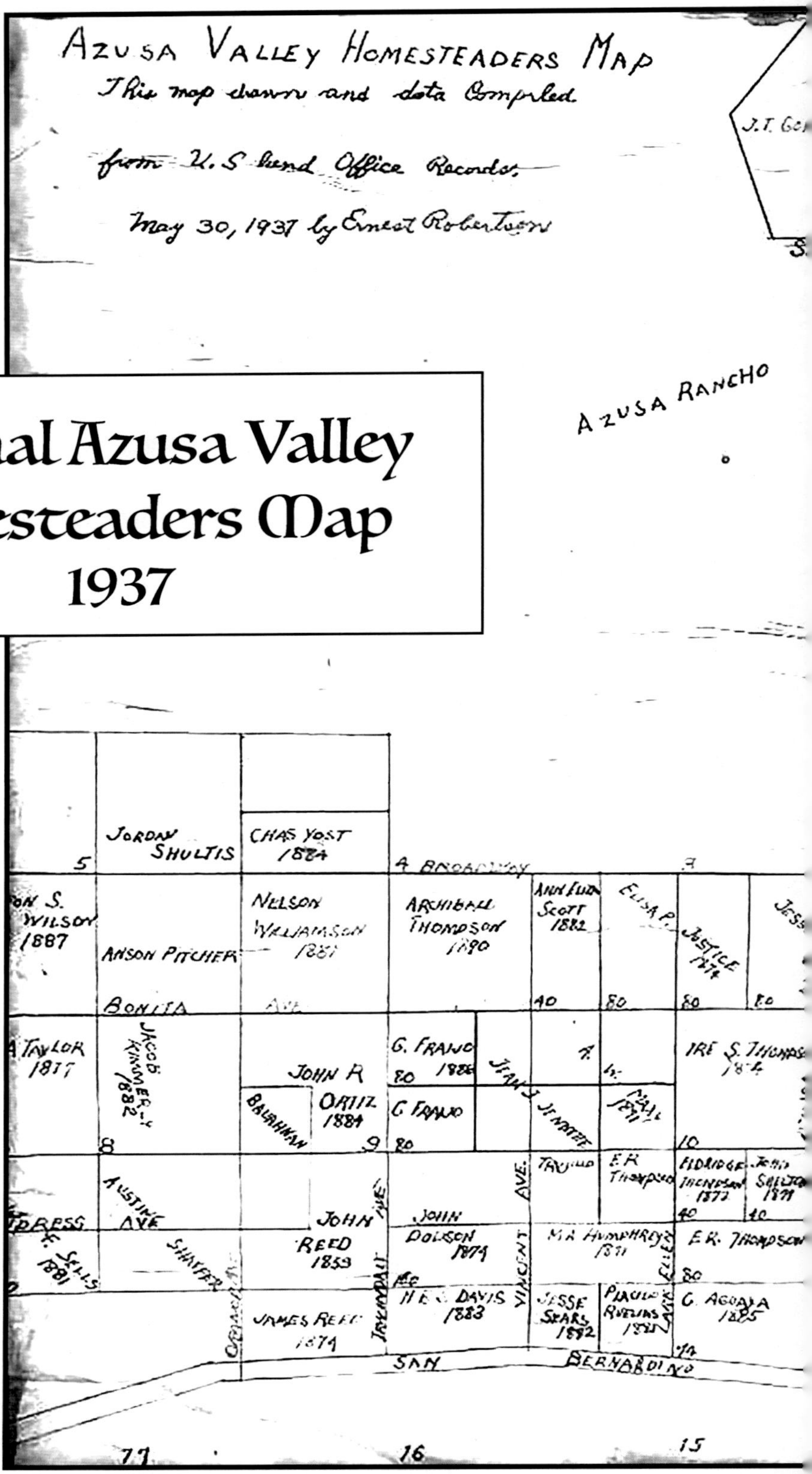

In 1937, Ernest Robertson created a map from Land Office records for the Azusa Valley Pioneer Society. It shows the homestead claims of the early pioneers, the earliest filed in 1865. Today it hangs in both the Azusa and Glendora Historical Museums.

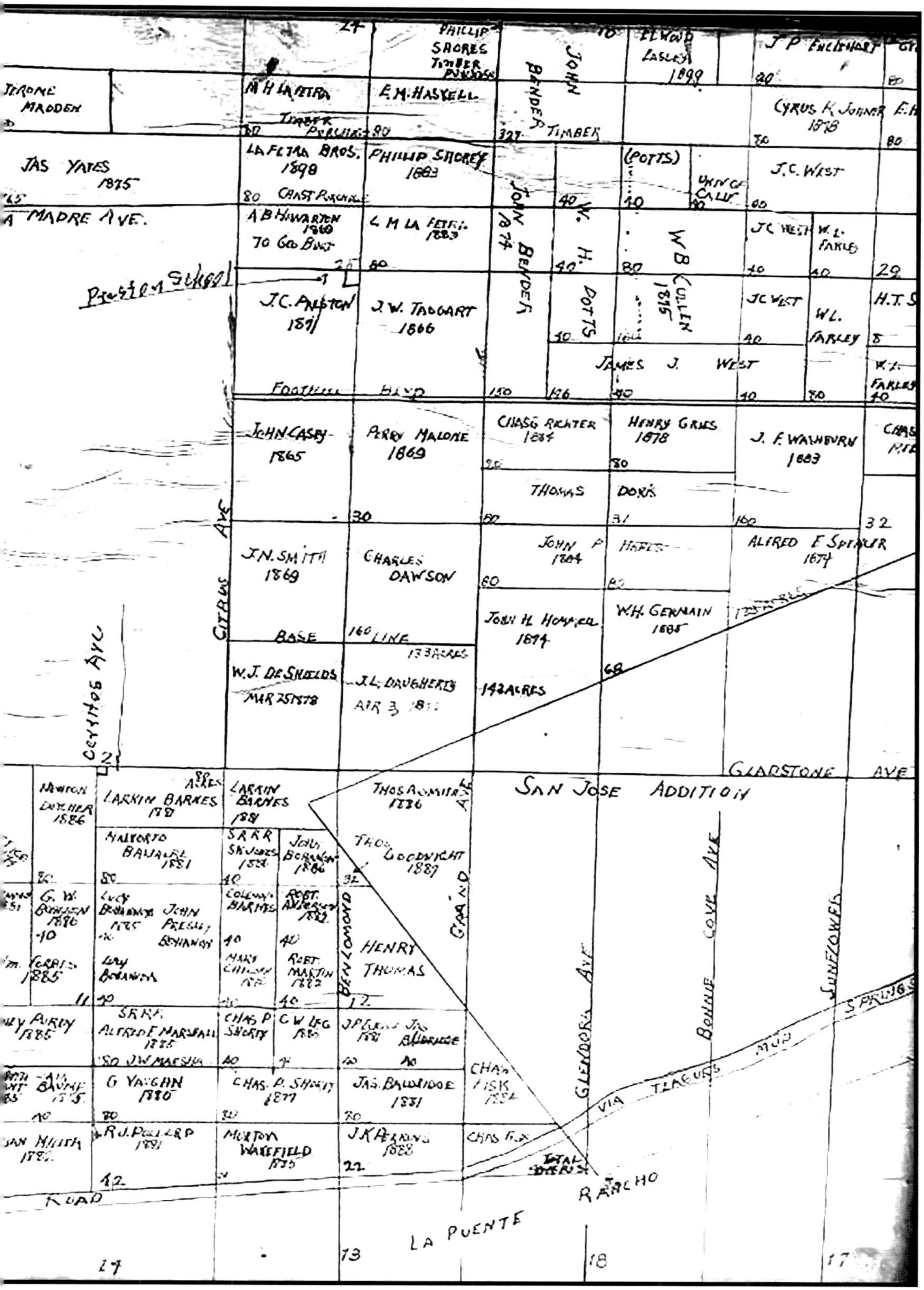

PHILLIP SHORES TIMBER PURCHASE
ELWOOD LASLEY 1899
J P ENGLEHART
JOHN BENDER TIMBER
JEROME MADDEN
M H LA FETRA
E.M. HASKELL
CYRUS K JOHNER 1878
JAS YATES 1875
LA FETRA BROS. 1898
PHILLIP SHOREY 1883
(POTTS)
UNIV OF CALIF
J.C. WEST
MADRE AVE.
A B HAWARTON 1869
L M LA FETRA 1883
JOHN BENDER 1874
W. H. POTTS
W B CULLEN 1875
JC WEST
W.L. FARLEY
Preston School
J.C. PRESTON 1871
J.W. TAGGART 1866
JAMES J. WEST
FOOTHILL BLVD
JOHN CASEY 1865
PERRY MALONE 1869
CHAS G RICHTER 1884
HENRY GRIES 1878
J. F. WASHBURN 1883
THOMAS DORR
J.N. SMITH 1869
CHARLES DAWSON
JOHN P HEFES 1884
ALFRED F SPENCER 1874
JOHN H. HOMMER 1874
W.H. GERMAIN 1885
BASE LINE
W.J. DE SHIELDS
143 ACRES
CITRUS AVE
CERRITOS AVE
GLADSTONE AVE
SAN JOSE ADDITION
LARKIN BARNES
THOS GOODNIGHT 1887
HENRY THOMAS
GRAND AVE
BEN LOMOND
GLENDORA AVE
BONNIE COVE AVE
SUNFLOWER
G. VAUGHN 1880
CHAS. P. SHOREY 1877
JAS. BALDRIDGE 1881
CHAS FISK
MORTON WAKEFIELD
VIA TLAGUAS
MUD SPRINGS
ROAD
RANCHO
LA PUENTE

Homesteaders

John Casey and William Jasper De Shields

News clip of John and Sarah Casey, c. 1865

William Jasper De Shields, c. 1865

Pioneer chic included beards. John Casey braided his whiskers and tucked them into his collar when he worked at a bench under the shade of an oak tree making oak and rawhide chairs. His daughter Frances claimed that she had never seen her husband Bill without his beard. So when I envision these two settlers fighting Dalton for water in the 1860s, I see beards and fists flying as they all shout insults over a muddy ditch. But mostly, I see beards.[1]

John Casey and his son-in-law William Jasper De Shields were two of the first white settlers in the Azusa Valley. Both of them rented land and water rights from Ranchero Henry Dalton.[2] Both filed claims on 160 acres apiece after the U.S. government surveyed their land and deemed it public property, and both were named, with a few other settlers, in Dalton's 1869 lawsuit against the homesteaders.[3] The court battle lasted years.

The early settlers were optimistic, though, about the trek to California, and Casey's story is typical of them. He moved from Plano, Texas, in 1857 in answer to a national call to move west. He got an urge, according to his daughter's account. Prompted by California lore touting the new state as a paradise, he knew fertile land was being offered for homesteading. So how could he resist? He was a farmer and stockman in Texas where there was a drought. Dallas was an unincorporated town of only about seven hundred people. Poor irrigation, no rail connection to other towns, and no market for whatever crops the Caseys could grow added to his desire to leave. The Civil War loomed over the southern states, too, and many settlers wanted to avoid it. Besides, Casey's family had already moved west more than once and knew the appeal of starting over.

His parents were from North Carolina and moved to Jackson, Tennessee, where John was born in 1810. Two years later, they moved to Arkansas where he was raised, attended school, and married. Then in 1844, he moved with his wife, young family, and parents to Texas. Again, they moved west. By the time his family set off for California, he was already forty-seven, his wife Sarah Nixon Thornburg, thirty, and they had three children: John Walter (15), Sarah Ellen (12), and Katherine Frances (7).

It took a year to prepare for the trip. His wife needed time to grow and dry fruit and beans and to sew extra clothes for her family. They needed barrels to fill with water from springs or rivers along the way, and they packed alcohol which was used for home remedies, for example, to treat cattle that suffered snakebites or wandered into alkaline water. When the Caseys packed up their wagon in Plano to go to California, there was no guarantee they'd reach their destination.

It wasn't a trip to make alone. They joined a wagon train because there was a danger of Apache Indian attacks, among other dangers. By the time the Caseys got on the Southern Route through Yuma and the desert sand dunes, travelers had written guide books, so they would have known the route between Yuma near Mexicali and Warner Ranch in San Diego County was popular and that the owner of the ranch catered to the needs of pioneers. Their main covered wagon was drawn by oxen, and John Jr. drove a light wagon pulled by horses. Many of the open prairies they crossed had no trees to use for firewood for the evening meal, so the children were given the chore of finding buffalo chips, dried rounds of buffalo dung that they could burn for fuel. A campfire required more than three bushels of chips. As long as they were dry, the chips burned like charcoal without an odor. The ideal place for a wagon train to camp was a site that had fuel, water, and grass for the work animals.

Two events along the route were memorable. One hot day, the Caseys came upon two men lying in the meager shade of some sagebrush. They were delirious from heat exhaustion and dehydration but recovered after a few days of care. They said they had had a disagreement with some of the members of the previous wagon train and had been left on the desert without food or water. It wasn't uncommon to pass graves along the trail.

On another occasion, John Jr. took the light wagon to a spring to get water. While he was filling the barrels, he realized Indians were going to attack, so he cut the horses loose and made it safely back to the wagon train. But the Indians ripped the canvas off the wagon and burned it and its contents. The Caseys lost their Sunday best clothes and much of the dried food, but they were safe and ready to rest for a few days when they reached Warner Ranch. Then other members of the wagon train separated, and John Casey opted to take his family to El Monte, and later Duarte, where he farmed briefly. In 1864 Casey and his family arrived on the Azusa Rancho where he rented land from Henry Dalton.[4]

Old-timers believed the early settlers enjoyed infinite perfect days in the Azusa Valley. If you look up at the San Gabriel foothills on a day when the sky is cerulean blue with swirls of white clouds crowning mountain peaks, you'll have an idea how beautiful the land was in the 1860s. Let your mind add the lush greens of growth above natural underwater springs, and the siennas and yellow ochres of rocks and earth, and you'll start hearing valley sounds: the rustling of foliage in a light breeze, the quick thump of a critter jumping from one branch to the next, the whinnies of horses in sycamore or oak groves, and perhaps the groaning of wagon wheels with the shifting of weight on their carriages. The settlers believed they'd reached a destination where all things were possible and plans for health and well-being were full of promise.

William J. De Shields' route to the valley was similar to Casey's, but he had a different dream. A young man, De Shields happened into the valley in the aftermath of the Gold Rush still looking for gold and eventually planted citrus trees and started a nursery.

Born in Beach Grove, Tennessee, in 1838 to a family of French Huguenots (Protestants), he moved with his family to Arkansas where they lived until 1854 when they, too, responded to the appeal of the West. Using ox teams and a prairie schooner, a small covered wagon, they traveled by wagon train on the Oregon Trail, arriving in Hood River Valley in that state by fall. Only four months later, William Jasper and his family moved to northern California near the Sutter mines. After the mines closed in 1866, he started homesteading in the Azusa Valley.[5]

It's romantic to think Casey befriended young De Shields and encouraged him to start a relationship with his daughter. A relative who spent years researching the De Shields family history believed they may have known the Caseys in Arkansas before the move west. However events occurred, Bill De Shields married Katherine Frances Casey in 1867. He was twenty-nine; she was seventeen. They raised a family of six. Two other children died young.

Both De Shields and Casey were walking into the middle of Dalton's fight with the U.S. government when they rented or leased land from him. According to Sheldon Jackson's book, *A British Ranchero in Old California*, Dalton was happy to accommodate the earliest settlers and had a cordial relationship with them. It's impossible to write about the two men without adding the context of Dalton's story because he became their foe soon enough in the fight over land and water.

Briefly, Dalton purchased the Ranchos Azusa and San José on December 24, 1844. They were Mexican land grants. When the Mexican-American War ended with the Treaty of Guadalupe Hidalgo in 1848, the United States took formal possession of California and agreed to honor those grants. Congress requested surveys in 1851, and Dalton had the boundaries of his land confirmed. The government did honor the grants for a while, but bogus claims prompted new land surveys. A surveyor named Hancock did a fraudulent survey in 1858 and left out a section of land between Dalton's two ranchos, 18,000 acres of his most valuable land. Hancock declared it open land — open for homesteading by settlers. Today, the land is Glendora, and Casey filed a homestead claim in 1865 on the 160 acres now beneath Citrus College and Azusa Pacific University. The streets on its perimeter are Citrus, Foothill, Alosta, and Barranca.[6]

Though Dalton was respected, he owned all the land in sight and, more importantly, all the water coming down out of the San Gabriel foothills. Whatever rights to water the early settlers had negotiated, Dalton became more possessive of his ditches as more homesteaders moved onto his land. A few things complicated his social position. Dalton was an Englishman, not an American, and he was married to Maria Guadalupe Zamorano from a prominent Mexican family. He'd also supplied arms to the Mexican army during the war, as had other farmers.[7] His action would have provoked his new contemporaries.

Neither Casey nor De Shields intended to be a squatter. Records show that both men paid Dalton for land and water rights while Dalton was trying to confirm his holdings and before the influx of settlers played havoc with his land grants. He spent the rest of his life trying to establish the boundaries of his ranchos in court, and so, made opponents of the men who lived closest to him, men he was now calling *squatters*. With temporal distance, it's easy to see both sides of the battles over water. Dalton expected his tenants to honor his landowner rights, and the homesteaders needed water, believed it should be free, and thought the law was on their side. They had no reason nor desire to doubt a federal surveyor, however questionable his findings.

Despite hostile relations with his neighbors, Henry Dalton worked with the settlers in 1868 to build a brush and adobe school for the children who lived between his Azusa home and along the foothills to San Dimas. It was constructed at what is now the intersection of Pasadena Avenue and Fifth Street in Azusa. Mexican, Indian, and white children were all welcome, according to Jackson's *British Ranchero*, and the community made the school a social center. De Shields was elected a trustee, and he was the one to buy books, later boasting that he was "able to carry all of them under one arm."[8]

Another account suggests that Casey and Dalton shared a mutual respect. They were, after all, neighbors and men of about the same age, Dalton seven years older.

Winnall Augustin Dalton, Henry's son, writes in a letter about a situation that prompted Casey to seek help from the Daltons. A man named Strickland had been sent by his doctor to live with John Casey until he died. Casey got supplies from Henry Dalton and his wife every day and gave them updates on the man's condition. His death was imminent.

When Maria Guadalupe Dalton learned that the doctor had said that getting the man in a good sweat would cure him, she said she'd get him well. The next evening, she rubbed the sick man with ointment, heaped blankets on top of him, and put a pure silver piece in his mouth. When the silver was tarnished with mercury fumes, she'd replace it with a second silver piece and clean the first one. He lived, so she taught Casey how to prepare gruel for the invalid as he recovered.

The letter doesn't say why the El Monte doctor suggested that Strickland stay with Casey. Strickland may have been a friend, or Casey may have been doing the doctor a favor. But the story suggests that Casey had a reputation for compassion and dependability, two traits that proved invaluable to settlers who arrived later.

After this anecdote about shared concern for a dying man, Winnall writes, "Shortly after this Casey refused to pay his rents and account for supplies and 'jumped' the land he had been renting."[9] Winnall was surprised by Casey's disloyalty. In his letters, he also criticizes Strickland's brief attempt to homestead and questions the claim of a man named James Weddle Taggart whom he supposed to be Strickland's friend. Perhaps that was the case, but after Strickland disappears from valley records, Taggart is still on the 1880 census raising seven children with his wife Sarah Ellen, Casey's other daughter.

Family records go a long way toward explaining Casey's abrupt change in attitude. Daughter Frances told her story about the homesteading of Dalton Ranch this way: "This is where Uncle Johnny and Aunt Sally [Sarah] Casey were living when the United States government sent men to determine the boundaries of the Spanish Land Grants which included the Dalton Ranch. Uncle Johnny was curious as to what the men were up to and watched them day after day. The day they finished surveying, one of them came to him and said, 'Old Man, do you live near here?' Uncle Johnny answered yes, and pointed to his house. 'Well Old Man, your house is on government land. You are entitled to homestead it.' This was a happy day for the Casey Family and after the regular procedure connected with the granting of the homestead, they owned their home at last."[10] Their neighbors knew the Caseys as Aunt Sally and Uncle Johnny.

Meanwhile, water was king.

In a memoir, Emmet Dougherty discusses the fight between Dalton and the homesteaders. "And the thing I remember best throughout more than 65 years is water, water, water. We brought five gallons with us, and when it was gone we had to hitch up and drive after some more. When we first came, Mr. Dalton owned the water. The Caseys and the [De] Shields had bought their land from Dalton and the water rights with it. Two of us would go, well armed, and we'd just take the water. We'd stay on guard until we had all we wanted and then we'd let Mr. Dalton have it again. I didn't do anything but just be there, because I was a boy — but my father did. Trouble always threatened but I never saw any actual shooting."[11]

Dalton was claiming the rights to all the water on his land, and he had the main ditch coming down to his own home. When he bought the Rancho Azusa, he hired a *mayordomo*, a superintendent for his ranch, and twenty Mexicans and Indians to build a settlement: a ranch house, stables, granaries, and tannery pits. His livestock needed water. Of course, he grew crops — alfalfa, barley, corn, peppers, onions, and more. He had a vineyard, too. The complicated history of the fights between Dalton and the settlers over water is colorful. Men brandished pistols over his ditch. There were ambushes, and an anonymous letter urged Dalton to meet the devil. An attempt was made to fence in the flow of water, and fences were burned down, the water diverted. Meanwhile more settlers arrived, and children were born.

The fights got old, and the settlers found a way to respect Dalton but also claim power over the ditches. They went to the government and requested a water district so they could control water in an equitable way — with their votes. The Los Angeles County Board of Supervisors founded the San José Water District in March 1871, the date of the first entry in a water ledger found in a storage cellar in Glendora in 2009. The book tells an interesting story.[12]

The minutes start with a request that a ditch be constructed across Dalton land. John Casey, his son John Walter, his son-in-law William Jasper De Shields, and other settlers — Griswold, Daugherty, Preston, Shorey, and West among them — were all on the Board of Water Commissioners: San José and Azusa Townships between 1871 and 1888.

The ledger is an account of the settlers' attempts to regulate the use of water in the valley, to secure the ditches for public use, and to provide water equitably to the growing agricultural community. Minutes from the meetings prove the settlers used scrip to sell water. They settled disputes in courtrooms both in Pomona and Los Angeles, and they paid *zanjeros* to regulate the flow of water and collect money for its use. *Zanjeros* were hired men who rode horseback along the ditches, checking the water flow, opening or closing gates to adjust its route, and chasing away those who had no right to the water. The settlers made efforts to behave responsibly, but Dalton's larger fight with the government over his land kept their relationships tenuous.[13]

Dalton fought the water district until the case reached the State Supreme Court in 1873 and again in 1874. Both times, the court decided in his favor, but both times the commission retained control because the ruling was difficult to enforce. The distance from Sacramento to the Azusa Valley was considerable on horseback. Another lawsuit against the commission in 1876 ruled for the settlers. After that, the commission granted Dalton forty percent of the water but charged him for it. Dalton was understandably angry and frustrated. The fighting continued, and Casey was leading the settlers.

Casey seems villainous in Dalton's biographies, but he was a respected leader. In addition to supporting the settlers in their fight for water, the Caseys also played a role in the organization and building of the first church in the valley. The earliest religious gatherings were held in sycamore or oak groves and were led by itinerate preachers. The Caseys provided land for at least one of the 1872 camp meetings. Then they opened their home in 1878 and 1879 to Southern Methodist organizers, including their friends the Doughertys, who wanted to build a church. Later, Casey gave an acre of his land on the east side of Citrus Avenue for the building. According to Polley Dougherty's memoir, a frame church was built there, property of the Methodist Episcopal Church South, and the Glendora M.E. church grew out of the Sunday School that was held there. An attempt was made to move the building closer to Azusa, but while it was on its underpinnings in December 1891, it was destroyed in an historic windstorm.[14] As Catholics, the Daltons attended Sunday services at the mission.

Though no one knew what the result of Dalton's lawsuit would be, Casey's family was growing in the 1870s and controlled much of the

Below: Katherine Frances Casey De Shields on the right, c. 1870

Katherine Frances Casey De Shields and unidentified child, c. 1869

W.J. and Katherine Frances Casey De Shields' children, c. 1900. Emma Alice (seated), (l-r) John Walter, Louis Martin, Mattye, Charles Francis, and Robert Casey.

disputed land. As his health failed, Casey deeded over twenty-four acres east of Citrus Avenue to his son John Walter who started planting walnut trees in 1871. Casey sold another 95 acres to the Wright family for $800. The court ruled in favor of the settlers in 1881, and finally in 1882, Casey received his homestead deed, a copy now hanging in the Glendora museum, the original in the Azusa museum.[15]

On the De Shields' land southeast of Casey, William Jasper and his wife, Casey's daughter Katherine Frances, planted an orange grove in 1874 with fruit and seeds he'd purchased in Los Angeles. The trees were irrigated from ditches that brought water from the San Gabriel River. Men on horseback made sure each rancher got his share. De Shields made extra cash by going into the San Gabriel Canyon to chop wood that he sold to settlers since wood was the only fuel used for cooking and heating at that time.

He started a nursery in 1878. According to his obituary, it became "world famous for oranges and lemons." He sold out to Dougherty, Hall, and others. If there was no name change, W.J. De Shields' business was Glendora Citrus Nurseries, as it appears in Hall's ads in Citrus High School annuals.[16]

The Gladstone House at 960 E. Gaillard St. in Azusa was the De Shields home. The Title Search Report lists Wm. De Shields as the homesteader of this house and land on March 24, 1878, confirming family stories of citrus groves and the large, old house with a porch

William Jasper De Shields family, c. 1902

around it. The title report goes on to say that James L. Dougherty bought twenty-five acres in 1883, after the Dalton loss, then sold twenty-three acres to the Gladstone Improvement Company which defaulted on the loan and sold back to Dougherty in 1889. The Gladstone company did not build the house and owned it only briefly. The home was large enough for the six De Shields children: Emma Alice (b. 1869), John Walter (b. 1874), Charles Francis (b. 1878), Louis Martin (b. 1880), Robert Casey (b. 1882), and Mattye (b. 1887).[17]

Casey's other daughter, Sarah Ellen, was James Weddle Taggart's third wife. He was a veteran of the Mexican-American War, having served under his father, Captain James Taggart, and was a founding member of the Veterans of the Mexican War in Los Angeles. He was born in Indiana in 1824, then settled in Oregon from 1852 to 1858 and traveled back and forth all his life. James W. was both a farmer and a miner. He and his wife settled northeast of Casey and were raising ten children by 1887.[18]

Casey's son John Walter was a farmer and horticulturist living on acreage from his father's original homestead. He served as the water commissioner from 1871 to 1878 for the Azusa and San José Townships. He and his wife Martha J. Boswell had four children: Mary Nixon, Lorena F., John Ransome, and Walter T.

John and Sarah Casey had almost twenty grandchildren on neighboring homesteads by the time Dalton's lawsuit ended, and other settlers' families had grown, too. Family members married into each other's families, and names changed. Many stayed in Glendora or neighboring towns, and there are descendants of both Casey and De Shields in Oakdale Cemetery. Few left Glendora. Those who did leave returned to visit with family or attended the pioneer picnics, another way of seeing family.

From 1922 to 1973, the Memorial Day picnics unified and celebrated the early communities. Most participants were the children and grandchildren of the original settlers. Unofficially, the group called itself the Pioneers of the Azusa Valley which included the entire area from El Monte east of the river and north to the mountains. It was all known as the Azusa Valley. The picnic group was renamed in 1929 to be inclusive of numerous towns. The Old Settlers Association of the Upper San Gabriel Valley created a Board of Trustees with a representative from each town. The first Board representatives were Charles West, Glendora; Charles Griffiths, Covina; Nancy Ward, Azusa; Mae Coffman, Baldwin Park; George Wright, Glendale; and out-of-valley districts. Before trains changed the landscape in 1887, the early settlers expected to travel distances to do business or visit friends, and it was to their advantage to be inclusive.

In addition to being a social gathering, the pioneer picnic group took on tasks for the community. In the late 1930s, the group took over care of the Fairmount Cemetery whose land was given to the people by J.C. Preston in 1871. About the same time Ernest Robertson, who served as the first president of the organization, created a pioneer map from Land Office Records on display in the Azusa museum. Finally, the group dedicated a Memorial Marker to the early pioneers that's in front of Azusa City Hall. The tribute was discussed for about ten years before volunteers found an appropriate boulder in the west fork of the San Gabriel Canyon, got permission from the Azusa City Council to place it, and orchestrated ceremonies for its installation. Nancy Ward wrote the inscription:

DEDICATED TO THE MEMORY
OF THE AZUSA VALLEY PIONEERS.
THEIR VISION, VIGILANCE,
AND VIRTUE ESTABLISHED A
PROSPEROUS COMMUNITY.
MAY THEIR INDOMITABLE SPIRIT
FOREVER INSPIRE POSTERITY.
ERECTED BY THE
AZUSA VALLEY PIONEER SOCIETY
MAY 30, 1932

Memorabilia from the picnic group was donated to the Azusa Public Library and was housed there and in the historical museum behind it. Attrition ended the picnic organization in 1973, and funds from the group were divided between the Azusa and Glendora Historical Societies.[19]

When John Casey and William Jasper De Shields arrived in this valley in the early 1860s, there were no towns called Azusa or Glendora. There were no streets, no homes, and no public services. There were Mexicans, Indians, and an Englishman named Henry Dalton on two vast ranchos: Rancho Azusa and Rancho San José.

By the time Casey and De Shields descendants created their own American dreams in the early 1900s, the valley was all citrus orchards, packing houses, and pepper trees — a gorgeous place to spend a childhood, as my grandmother felt lucky to have done. A feisty woman with an eye for fashion, she disliked her grandfather's beard and its tendency to catch food. She emphasized in her memoir that when William Jasper De Shields passed away on July 24, 1917, in Norwalk and was laid out for burial, his beard was on top of the sheet.

The Oregon Whitcombs
George Bennett and Meda Ella

Meda Ella Shepperd, Kansas, 1884

George Bennett Whitcomb, c. 1900

No one remembers George Bennett Whitcomb or his wife. No one recalls the excitement of their arrival in Glendora from Kansas in 1886. Nothing remains of them but the names on Bennett and Meda avenues, and maybe a ruined monument in Fairmount Cemetery, noted on a website years ago.

Three of their four children are buried on an island in Green Peter Reservoir, Oregon. Campers in Whitcomb Creek Park on the opposite shore look out on a landscape that's perfect for canoes and kayaks. They don't know about the graves on Whitcomb Island, nor do they know those children were once mourned in Glendora, California.

Everyone in the San Gabriel Valley knows the Whitcomb name, though. George Bennett's father, George Dexter Whitcomb, laid out the town of Glendora, California, and made his home there with his wife Leadora and five of their six children.

By the time George Dexter arrived in California, he was already a successful businessman. Born in Vermont in 1834, he was raised and attended business college in Ohio. In 1856, he moved to Minnesota to work as a time clerk in a railroad company. There, he met and married Leadora Bennett in 1859. They moved to Chicago where he became a purchasing agent for a railroad. When he was rejected for volunteer military service due to childhood injuries, he did civilian duty by producing supplies for Union Army railroads during the Civil War. George Dexter was a businessman, a builder of bridges and steamboats, and a supplier of equipment, so he started his own business in Chicago in the early 1870s producing coal mining machinery and coal field supplies for railroads. Whitcomb Locomotive Works prospered under his leadership, then that of trusted employees, and later of his son William Card Whitcomb and son-in-law William Dalzell.[1]

Throughout his career, George Dexter was dedicated to his family. He and Leadora had lost their second son before his first birthday, and when two other children had health issues, they looked for a more temperate climate near Los Angeles. In 1884, he found and purchased several hundred acres on the former Dalton Rancho and started building his own home and the town of Glendora, named for both the glen behind his home and his wife's nickname, Dora. He put all his energy into his project. First, he made sure the Santa Fe railroad would run its newest line close to the new town. Then he formed the Glendora Water and Land Companies. The water company began preparing its facilities while the land company cleared land, and built homes, the Hotel Bellevue, and a Land Office. He gave land for the Methodist Church and a new school.[2]

Committed to his faith, Whitcomb's idealism was evident in the deed that new homeowners signed; it upheld moral principles and included a nondrinking clause. The prohibition created friction when a land speculator made a brief attempt to start a town called Alosta just south of Whitcomb's property, but George Dexter's vision prevailed. He wanted to lay out a Christian town, in other words, a civilized town, and he didn't want bars or saloons near young families.[3] Today his idealism seems rigid, but California was a wilderness to the settlers who arrived in the 1880s. Glendora became an oasis for them.

It had been only about sixty years since Mexico had taken control of California from the Spanish and from the Catholic missions, and only about thirty years since the Mexican-American War ended. The multi-ethnic population of Los Angeles, like the rest of the southern part of the state, was Spanish, Mexican, and Native Californian, and they were mostly Catholics who spoke Spanish.[4] In addition, the population had many transients. Sailors on merchant ships from other countries had been sharing goods up and down the coast for decades, usually near mission lands. Adventurers were still looking for gold, and the boom of the 1880s brought many wanderers into the state. Understandably, Whitcomb wanted an environment that would feel familiar to young families, the root of the words *family* and *familiar* calling attention to an inherent desire for commonalities. It was the best of both worlds to have a culturally rich world around a small, family-centered town where youthful settlers could exercise their optimism and energy.

But the founding of a town is a huge undertaking. Of course, Whitcomb would have wanted his eldest son, George Bennett to help him in this new enterprise. His son shared his technical skills and had completed his college education in Chicago where the 1880 census finds him at nineteen living with the entire Whitcomb family and two Swedish servants. He was a single surveyor. How George Bennett went from Chicago to Kansas to marry remains a mystery, but the Kansas State Census Collection 1885 shows him at twenty-six living in Wabaunsee County, Kansas, a married farmer whose wife's family lived on a nearby farm. He married seventeen-year-old Meda Ella Shepperd of Kansas on November 4, 1883. Their son George Ernest Whitcomb was born in 1886, the year the young family took a train west to help with the building of Glendora. George Bennett's plan was to work as a contractor and builder for his father, and he did that for about three years. He was a young man seeking to prove himself. Meda's family was to follow them west at the end of the next year.

Meda Ella was a beautiful young woman. A family picture shows her corseted and hopeful in a dress worthy of Kansas belles. Yet, there she was at twenty on a westward bound train with a baby on her lap and no disposable diapers. She was leaving her family, her reliable child-care, in Kansas.

In Glendora, George Dexter Whitcomb was laying out the streets. He named the east-west roads after family members — one for Meda his new daughter-in-law and another for Bennett his son — and the north-south streets after the states from which new homeowners had traveled west. It was a kind gesture to welcome Meda Ella by naming a street after her, and she must have enjoyed the excitement in this new town. Vista Bonita was still the main street, but businessmen were starting to move to Michigan (Glendora) Avenue, a short walk from the train depot.[5] George Dexter lined the streets with pepper trees. The Bellevue Hotel was also finished that year in honor of the coming of the Santa Fe railroad, and it was on one of the first of these trains to stop at the Glendora station that the Shepperd family arrived on December 2, 1887.[6]

They adapted quickly. Jennie and Jacob set up a boarding house, while daughter Meda and her family lived next door to Dr. August and Rosa Engelhardt on Whitcomb between Vista Bonita and Wabash.[7] Four of the six children — Frank (16), Olive (14), Maggie (12), and Cora (8) — attended Whitcomb school.[8] Their first two teachers were Mr. Sykes and Prof. Eden, the latter living with his wife in Meda Ella and George Bennett's house. The eldest Shepperd son, William Russell, was still in Kansas and would join them later.[9]

Meda Ella and her husband George Bennett didn't stay in Glendora to witness either the growth of the town or their respective families. George Bennett needed someplace to exercise his skills out of his father's shadow. He too had a town to plot. He had streets to name and businesses to run, and he longed for a more pristine environment. The Oregon version of his story says he was lured north by a tale of elk with horns six-to-eight feet wide and timber so thick that a man had to turn sideways to walk between the trees. He went north to see how the elk — with their legendary breadth — did it.[10]

But I bet Meda Ella didn't want to go. She had sisters and a mother in Glendora to help raise her young family, and she could help them. Her son Walter was born on May 5, 1888. She had just moved from Kansas to California, and the distance north to Lebanon, Oregon, with two boys under three would have seemed infinite — even by train.

No matter what George Bennett and his wife were feeling, the establishment of the Whitcomb post office on a butte of land in Linn County, Oregon, on December 26, 1889, dated their arrival. It was in service until May 15, 1899, and George Bennett ran it himself. He was the one to carry mail on horseback from Foster to the miners near his new home. The opening of the post office was the beginning of the town of Whitcomb.

George Bennett loved the rugged beauty of the mountains near the confluence of the Santiam River and Quartzville Creek. Quartzville was an old gold mining and boom town, and gold dust was legal tender when the family arrived. The Big Bottom area had huge timber stands and an abundance of wild game. To reach the Whitcomb homestead from Lebanon required traveling by team and wagon to the end of the road, then by horseback and foot to the home site. George Bennett homesteaded 160 acres of land, later purchasing another 160 acres, and he went to work mining, logging, building, and farming.[11]

The first Whitcomb house was a log cabin that burned down in 1912. Plans for a new house with fourteen or fifteen rooms to serve as an inn were never completed because, by then, travel to and from the Quartzville mines had dwindled. The homestead included a barn for his forty or fifty head of cattle. Acreage was set aside for hay and an orchard, and a fruit drier was built for apples and pears. Elk and venison were plentiful. In fair weather, itinerate ministers or neighbors held Sunday services under a maple tree in an open-air church on the land. George Bennett made a pulpit and benches for it. Meda Ella had a violin and a cornet, and when she found people to play them, the Whitcombs would move the benches to one side and host square dances there.[12]

His college education made George Bennett a valued leader of the community, according to Roy Elliott who wrote a profile of the Whitcomb family in 1971 for his book *Profiles of Progress*. Once George Bennett's homestead was established, he turned to public works. He supervised the construction of Big Bottom Road that began in 1903. The work was slow and grueling because there was no equipment — only horses and manpower. He added personal funds to public ones to continue the road between the trees, and when it was completed, he opened a stagecoach line from Lebanon to Cascadia.

Whitcomb set up an assay office and mined near the river with Gwinn, his neighbor. The attempt failed because they tried mining too extensively for the amount of water they had, but he found platinum there. He also took pack horses from Whitcomb to Quartzville where mining was done along the creek. He mined copper and silver in the Paywell Mine that he owned. Its 200-foot tunnel is under the roadway today, and the old miners' cabins along Quartzville Creek are now used for fishing and outings.

George Bennett Whitcomb (r) with packers and hunters on trail from Whitcomb to Quartzville, Oregon, c. 1900

George Bennett set up a logging company, too. Local homesteaders found they could make a profit by clearing fir trees from their own land, but the logging could occur only in areas near a stream large enough to float the logs to the mill in Lebanon. It was a cumbersome process best done in the spring when the water level was high.[13]

Pictures taken by an amateur photographer show that Oregon life wasn't easy on the Whitcomb homestead. I can identify only Meda Ella, though George Bennett may be one of the men, and a young boarder named Kate Marinan may be the woman helping Meda iron. In one picture, the subjects are canning fruit. In another, a man holds a knife to an upended pig that's been gutted. Two other pictures feature wash day. The land was isolated, accessible only by a trail, and it was fourteen miles to the nearest wagon road. Here on the Whitcomb homestead near Sweet Home and Lebanon, Meda Ella and George Bennett had two more children, Arella and Leadora. And it was here that the three youngest children — eleven, seven, and six years old — died during an outbreak of diphtheria in 1899, the year George Bennett closed the post office.

Whitcomb homestead, Oregon, 1909.
Meda Ella (r) and maybe boarder, Kate Marinan, ironing.

Meda Ella Whitcomb (r), maybe George Bennett, and boarder Kate Marinan, 1909, butchering pig.

Meda Ella Whitcomb (l) with unidentified man and woman, wash day on Whitcomb homestead, 1909

Meda Ella Whitcomb (r), unidentified men, maybe boarders, canning.

Meda Ella Whitcomb, son Ernest (standing), and baby Walter, Glendora, 1889

George Ernest Whitcomb, Lebanon, Oregon, c. 1894

Even worse than the parents' agony must have been Ernest's sorrow. He was only twelve or thirteen as he watched his brother and two sisters succumb to the contagious bacterial infection that attacks a victim's throat, making it difficult to breathe or talk. At the time, there was no vaccine for the disease, medical aid some distance away, and he watched and perhaps helped his father dig the graves not far from their home. When he was interviewed at eighty-two, he still found it difficult to talk about their deaths.

I have a letter that my great-grandmother Maggie De Shields wrote to her sister from Glendora on October 24 of that year. It's addressed to Mrs. Ella Whitcomb in Foster, Oregon. I'm including about half the letter on the next page because it says so much about being a woman in Glendora in 1899. A few notes about it: Maggie's children were Frances, Bob, and Glen. Her husband Walter's elderly parents had sold their Glendora citrus nursery and moved to Norwalk to live next door to their eldest daughter. Cora Shepperd was living in Los Angeles. The Snavely family lived in Glendora and attended old-timer picnics for years. William Shepperd's wife was named Alice, nicknamed Allie. The spelling errors are Maggie's.

Dear Sister

You see by the date of this letter that I am 24 yrs. old today. And also by the scratches on this paper that one of the children have been using a led pencil freely. I spent about three weeks at Walter's folks this summer & had a fine time. I took the children & went to see Cora last Monday & stayed until Thursday morning. I got most of our winter under clothes while I was there and came home with my heels blistered and a corn on one toe. Cora lives about three quarters of a mile from the main part of town and it was quite a job to push the baby buggy up and back every day.

I got some cheap pictures taken of Frances and Bobbie. I will send you two of each & you can divide with Allie the first time you get a chance.

I suppose you remember Mr. Snavely — He died today about noon. I believe he had consumption. Such happenings brings our minds to you and your trouble. I have tryed to sympathize with you — I have turned my thoughts every way. I know I felt bad & yet I feel that nothing — nothing but the same sad experience would make me to fully realize just how you feel.

How I wish you could be with us. We would all try so hard to keep your mind from that which we know you think of most. But I must not say any more for I feel so very incompotent [sic] to do you any good.

Howard Glen is a nice baby but we have quite a great deal of trouble with getting milk to agree with him. He is smaller than either of the other two children. He is three months old & weighs only 1/2 pound more now than Bobbie did when he was born.

I did a big washing this morning & I expect I will have another about Friday — I have to wash twice a week since my family has increased. I dont do any thing but cook, eat, wash dishes, wash and iron. Oct 27.

I have ironed and washed since I started this letter and will iron again tomorrow.

I have got me a new (secondhand) baby buggy. . . .

With much love to all from your sister.

Maggie

She wouldn't have known that consumption was a common illness from 1870 into the early 1900s as sick easterners moved west to improve their health.

Meda Ella Whitcomb, c. 1911

George Ernest Whitcomb, c. 1902

I have other letters that were sent to Meda Ella between 1899 and 1924. They're full of trivia about both Glendora and George Bennett's family: It was dusty and dry in 1903 when Jennie Shepperd wrote to ask her daughter Ella to visit and bring the rain with her. Carroll Whitcomb left apples with the Shepperds for his brother's family, and Jennie offered solutions to Ella's financial problems. She told her daughter she could sew with her mother's help while she visited them in Glendora, and Ella's son Ernest could earn money for the return trip to Oregon by helping her husband Jacob with janitorial work at the school, probably the Whitcomb School. In 1905, the Whitcombs traveled north to visit George Bennett and his family.

George Ernest was working on his degree in mining at Oregon Agricultural School from 1905 to 1909. In 1907 his aunt Maggie and her husband Walter were trying to get out of a Glendora business partnership in a mercantile store so they could start a business for themselves on Michigan Avenue. They would have to sell their house and lot to accomplish this. An advertisement for J.W. De Shields' store ran in the 1908 Citrus High School annual, and the dentist upstairs from their market was Glenn Odell.

In a letter dated 1909, Maggie shares that the house they've been living in has burned down. Glendorans came to the rescue and saved all but one box of pictures whose loss Maggie and her daughter Frances regretted for the rest of their lives. The De Shields family found shelter in rooms over the Land Company office and did their cooking in the room behind their store. If my grandmother's memory of Glendora was accurate in the 1980s when we toured the town, the house that burned stood where the historical museum stands now. Their market was on the west side of the street at about 211 Glendora (Michigan) Ave.

Of course, there's more information in both the letters and public records. Ernest Whitcomb earned a degree in mining engineering in 1909, made land and location surveys, and was the City Engineer for Lebanon, Oregon, for twenty years. Meda Ella and George Bennett had marital problems in 1914. Ella was doing "the sencible thing," according to her sister Maggie who referred to more "troubles" in a 1916 note. She used the word often to indicate everything from health concerns to financial stress but was reluctant to identify personal problems in her letters or diary. The Federal Census of 1920 shows Meda Ella divorced and living with her sister Maggie and family in Los Angeles. George Bennett died in 1921 and is buried in California. The 1930 census shows Meda Ella living back in Lebanon, Oregon, where she died that year at sixty-four. She lived a much shorter life than her sister Maggie who died at ninety-six and her son Ernest who lived to ninety. At his death in 1976, Ernest left two daughters, seven grandchildren, twenty great-grandchildren, and five great-great-grandchildren. Quite a legacy for the only child to survive an outbreak of diphtheria.

In 1967, the creation of Green Peter Dam turned the former Whitcomb homestead and cemetery into an island. On the opposite shore, Whitcomb Creek County Park offers campsites and facilities for boating, fishing, and outdoor sports. The Whitcomb name appears often — on a boat ramp, a bridge, the park, the island, and the creek — but only history buffs know there was once a town of Whitcomb with its own post office. Now it's under the sparkling waters of the lake.

Glendora's monument to the children is also long gone. The Whitcombs and Shepperds probably held a memorial service in the pioneer cemetery in 1899 when their grief was fresh. Their neighbors the Englehardts would have been there, perhaps with the Cullens and Benders. The Kamphefner relatives would have attended, as would whichever Caseys still lived in Glendora. The Inman branch of the De Shields family tree would have come by horse and wagon from Norwalk. And there would have been friends — the Doughertys, Odells, Prestons, Clardys, perhaps the Shoreys, and Wests — all named in either my great-grandmother's letters or my grandmother's memoir. All of Glendora would have gathered on the hill to pay tribute to the Whitcomb children.

1895 Linking Pioneer Genes

Mary Margaret Shepperd and John Walter De Shields

Newlyweds Mary Margaret Shepperd and John Walter De Shields with their wedding gifts displayed behind the couple. July 3, 1895.

One of my Glendora friends is mystified by the good feeling there is in San Gabriel Valley towns, especially her own. She often questions whether it's the air or the water that makes her feel so contented to live in such a comforting place. The sense of well-being she tries to describe defies words, but I've felt it myself and am equally mystified by it. I have an advantage, though, because I attended the pioneer picnics for the first twenty years of my life and know the camaraderie and love that was established early in this area. Lifestyle bound the early settlers together.

The secretary's handwritten minutes of the pioneer picnic meetings are evidence, but though the picnics were held from 1922 to 1973, only the last ledger remains in the Azusa Historical Museum where it was found in 2008. The earlier three or four ledgers have been missing for over fifty years, probably squirreled away in an attic or closet somewhere in the valley.

My great-grandmother Maggie De Shields spent forty-four years recording them. She was elected for life to be the secretary of the Settlers of the East San Gabriel Valley and served from 1926 to 1970, the year before she died at ninety-six on Memorial Day 1971, the day of the annual picnic.

You might well ask why any of this is important. Why impose significance on a death that synchronously happened on picnic day? Why search for old records?

My answer is this: Those records of the annual picnics symbolize and honor the spirit of the founding pioneers in this valley. The respect and joy these settlers shared annually set a precedent that our local towns are trying to maintain and expand today. They record the cohesive and energetic spirit that our founders brought with them when they ventured west, and today that spirit is still palpable when a soft breeze blows down from the foothills and calms the turmoil of the present. You can feel it.

Maggie De Shields was the ideal person to entrust with the history of the valley because her own huge family shared in it. Her marriage to Walter De Shields linked many of the original names in this area. On the De Shields side: the Caseys and Taggarts. And on the Shepperd side: the Whitcombs, Kamphefners, Cullens, and Engelhardts. Many of them stayed in Glendora, as the names on the gravestones in Oakdale Cemetery show, and those who left returned each year to see friends and relatives at the picnics and other events like weddings.

Weddings are also celebrations of unity. Families are joined. Loyalty is sworn. Love is celebrated. Maggie Shepperd and Walter De Shields' wedding announcement paints a detailed picture of Glendora society in 1895. Not only did the writer describe the setting, the ceremony, and the procession, but he or she named participants and guests, and included a list of their gifts.

While I was volunteering in the Glendora museum, I speculated about the wedding with other volunteers who knew far more than I did about 1895. I'm including the announcement here, a newspaper clipping from an unidentified local newspaper, and some thoughts about our guesswork.

The Glendora Christian Church was the scene of another very pretty wedding last Wednesday evening, July 3, the contracting parties being Miss Maggie Shepperd and Mr. Walter DeShields, both of Glendora. The decorations of the church were under the direction of Miss Iola Wight and were arranged with very pretty effect. A large screen of pepper and oleander blossoms, with the monogram of the bride and groom in the center, divided the platform lengthwise.

The Glendora Guitar Club, of which the bride is a member, was concealed by this screen and played an appropriate selection as the bridal party proceeded up the aisle, also playing softly during the ceremony which was performed by Rev. F. A. Wight, the bride and groom standing under a floral umbrella made of ferns and yucca blooms. They left the church to the strains of the wedding march. The ushers were Messrs. Woodard Reynard and James Baker. The bride looked charming in a lovely gown of soft cream goods, trimmed with lace, and an effective garniture of orange blossoms and carried a bouquet of white carnations, tied with white satin ribbon.

After the ceremony an elegant wedding supper was served at the home of the bride's parents to the relatives and a few invited guests and a flash light picture was taken of the bridal party.

Mr. and Mrs. DeShields received a number of presents, useful and ornamental, of which the following is a list: Dishes, glassware, etc., from the bride's parents; hand towels and worsted quilt, Mr. and Mrs. DeShields, father and mother of the groom; set teaspoons, Mrs. Shepperd; bamboo table, Mr. and Mrs. F. Shepperd; painting of roses, Miss Emma Inman; engraving of "Good night," Mr. and Mrs. S. J. Miller; glass water set and tray, Mr. and Mrs. Beardslee; sugar shell, Mrs. Lydia E. Stone; salt and pepper dishes, Vivian Miller; silver standard, glass fruit dish, Daisy and Lewis Beardslee; set decorated cups and saucers, Mr. and Mrs. Thomas Kamphefner; set glass tumblers, Charlie DeShields; set table napkins, Mattie DeShields; glass olive dishes, Mrs. Chadwick; mustard dish, Bertie Chadwick; glass lamp, Wilbur George and John Grove; Japanese teapot, Mrs. Bradley; hand towels, Mrs. Hendrickson; sofa cushion, Mrs. and Misses Casey, of Pomona; table tray, Mr. and Mrs. J. White; stand table cover, M. Ray; button bag and music, Iola Wight; dessert spoon, Maude Shepperd; upholstered oak rocker from members of the Christian church.

The Christian Church was on the northeast corner of Wabash and Bennett in 1895, and the bride's parents, Jennie and Jacob Shepperd, lived in the Bradley house on North Vista Bonita.[1] The distance between the

Christian Church on the northeast corner of Wabash and Bennett

two locations is short. The bride and groom may have led the wedding party on foot or in a horse-drawn carriage from the church to the Shepperd home for supper. I doubt that beef was served. The family cow was too important.

In a meeting of the Glendora Historical Society in 1949, Maggie De Shields told her audience that her father had had a large garden in front of the schoolhouse. Jacob Shepperd used to tie his cow with a rope in front of the building where it ate the grass. When Maggie and Walter married, her parents mortgaged that cow for thirty-five dollars so the young couple could set up housekeeping — though they were afraid the cow would die before they got the cash.

The Shepperds may have chosen to have the wedding meal catered by the Glendora Hotel, but it's more likely that family members helped prepare the meal for the twenty or more guests. The entrée may have been chicken or ham. Game is a possibility, too, since Glendorans used to shoot quail and rabbits. Chickens would have been raised in town and plucked locally. According to Margaret House, once curator of the Glendora Historical Museum, there was a public area on Vermont in the 1890s where Glendorans used to stake their livestock, and many people had smokehouses that benefitted both family and friends. Some kind of meat would have been served.

There would have been special savories, perhaps oysters or caviar, nuts or dates. All these were available to Glendorans via the railroad from Los Angeles. At a July wedding, fruits and vegetables were plentiful, not to mention the canned goods that Glendorans stored. Mincemeat, for example, was preserved in rum or whiskey, so there may have been mincemeat pies. Cornmeal was a staple, and I found Maggie's 1895 recipe for corn cakes in a museum file. The wedding cake would have been a molasses, sponge, butter, or white cake. Or the family may have taken advantage of local orchards to make fruit fillings for pies. Thomas and Rosa (Engelhardt) Kamphefner were family and may have assisted in plans for the meal because they owned the grocery store on Vista Bonita. His brother Henry Kamphefner was married to Maggie's sister Olive Shepperd and lived on 160 acres in the canyon.

Their wedding gifts were displayed behind Maggie and Walter in the pictures. Members of the Christian Church gave them an oak rocker that had a place in their home until 1971 when Maggie passed away, Walter already gone. The painting of roses from Emma De Shields Inman, Walter's older sister, graced their living room. Some of the gifts were made by hand, like the quilt or painting. The hand towels may have been embroidered.

Most of the guests were relatives. The grooms' parents were William Jasper and Katherine Frances (Casey) De Shields. They homesteaded the 160 acres of land on the corner of Gladstone and Citrus, the property beneath the Gladstone House, and they started a nursery on that land in 1878.[2] Emma, Charlie, and Mattye De Shields were the groom's siblings. Emma was already married to Joe Inman who started the Norwalk Bank. It was her second marriage; she was widowed when Charles Miller passed away. Her daughter Vivian Miller was a child at the wedding. Brothers Robert and Louis aren't mentioned.

The groom's grandfather was John Casey, the first renter, then homesteader in the Azusa Valley. His land was the 160 acres where Citrus College is now. Casey's son John Walter had moved to Pomona with his family, so his wife Martha J. Boswell and their daughters, Mary Nixon and Lorena Frances Casey were the guests from Pomona.

Frank Shepperd, the bride's brother, and his wife Alice Chadwick are named in the article, as well as their firstborn Maude Shepperd, who was three at the time of the wedding but later died of peritonitis, still a child in Glendora. Maggie's other siblings aren't mentioned. Her sister Cora was probably there, as her sister Olive and her husband Henry Kamphefner would have been. Her brother William R. Shepperd is not mentioned, and her sister Meda Ella Shepperd was married and living with her husband George Bennett Whitcomb in Oregon where they were establishing a town. It would be four more years before they lost their three youngest children to diphtheria.

Pioneer families were close. It isn't a surprise that the Beardslees were still friends of the Caseys and De Shields, three families among the oldest in the valley.

Music clubs were popular in the 1800s, and young people were often photographed playing their favorite instruments. Guitars and pianos were preferred in the Shepperd family, and the sound of guitars being played in unison would have been a soothing addition to the wedding ceremony itself. If our ancestors wanted music, they had to learn to play a musical instrument. To cook required taking an ax to the wood supply, and to marry was to share bath water.

I can only speculate about the wedding night — and perhaps I shouldn't. My great-grandmother was a religious woman with a strong sense of propriety. As an elderly widow, she expressed an appreciation that she had found her wifely duties so pleasurable. I also know that there were shivarees in Glendora and that Maggie wasn't fond of them. A few years later, she was to hide her three children under the bed when men filled the streets, whooping and hollering and shooting off their guns in celebration of newlyweds. The shivaree tradition disappeared with frontier California. Originally, it was a lively serenade in honor of a young couple, but the western addition of guns made it a hostile custom. How the bride and groom were feted and where they spent the night are mysteries, but a month later my grandmother, Frances Porter De Shields was conceived, followed by brothers Robert William and Howard Glen, the latter named for Glenn Odell, the town dentist.

This wedding announcement was just the beginning of Maggie and Walter's family life. You've seen a photo of Walter De Shields if you know anything about the history of Glendora. Standing below the window of Glenn Odell's dental practice, he's the man at the left of a photograph of the Wood building. He and his wife Maggie owned and operated the general store behind the pepper tree and delivery wagon for about five years from 1905 to 1910. My grandaunt, Jean De Shields Bacchilega, identified her grandfather in this familiar picture, not from his grocer garb, his stance, or his sleeve garters, but by his hat with its circular brim, a style he wore most of his life. Prior to buying his own store, Walter was a partner in the G.W. Hall Mercantile Company, but the young couple mortgaged their home to set up their own grocery.[3]

My grandmother, Frances P. De Shields (later Patten, then Metzger), was full of tales of the store and recorded trivia about it in her memoirs. She mentions the hitching post that she swung on as a child, the pepper tree, the delivery boys, and the new telephone whose number was 81 on the sign in this picture and others of the Wood building.[4] The photo may have been taken in 1908, the year after Glenn Odell earned his degree in dentistry from USC, and the year J.W. De Shields ran an ad for his store in *La Palma* magazine, the Citrus High School annual. According to Donald Pflueger's book *Glendora*, there were 129 telephones in this town by 1907, and in her memoirs, Frances talks about the excitement of having phone service in the store.[5]

Maggie and Walter constructed a wall at the back of the grocery with a kitchen behind it so Maggie could serve lunch to her family when the three children came home from Whitcomb School. It was the same school Maggie had attended after the Shepperd family arrived from

J.W. De Shields Market, 1905-1910, with Walter De Shields on the left and upstairs the Odell dentistry, telephone 81

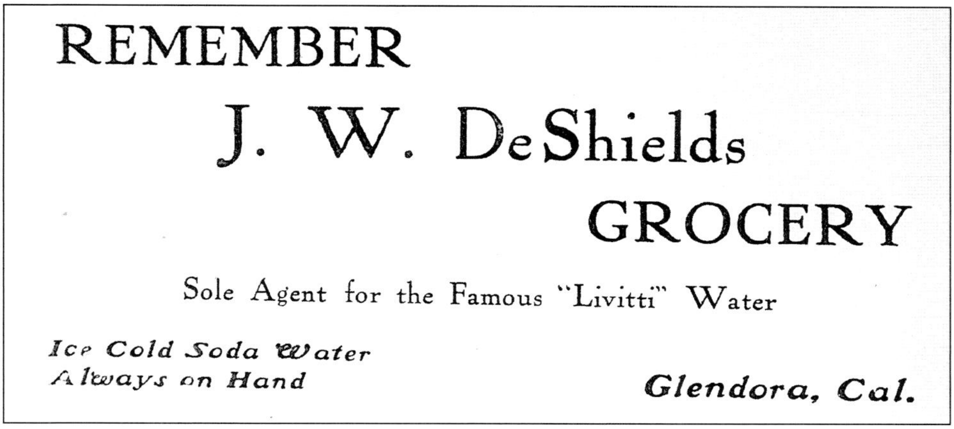
REMEMBER
J. W. DeShields
GROCERY
Sole Agent for the Famous "Livitti" Water
Ice Cold Soda Water
Always on Hand
Glendora, Cal.

An ad for J.W. De Shields grocery store in the La Palma, Citrus High School annual, 1908

Oil shack behind J.W. De Shields store, August 1923

Kansas in 1887.[6] Behind the store was an oil shack. Despite Whitcomb's objection to alcohol and his own wife's membership in the Women's Christian Temperance Union, Walter kept his hooch in the shack. In 1923 on a visit to relatives in Glendora, Maggie and Walter posed for a picture beside it, perhaps a humorous symbol of marital compromise.[7]

No doubt Walter found his wife's organizational skills daunting, but she learned to be patient with him, too. On the back of a young woman's picture in one of my family albums, my grandmother wrote, "Dad's whoop de doop." I'm not going to share her name, but long after Walter's death, my grandmother and her mother sometimes discussed the girl who sat on Walter's lap in the store and took money out of the till — if there was money in it. Maggie said the women of the Christian Church wanted to ban this other woman from religious services in a show of camaraderie with her, but Maggie wouldn't let them. She insisted that churches are built for sinners and no one should be banned from a church.

On a miscellaneous note, daughter Frances once asked her father what the difference was between the coffee in the expensive barrel and the coffee in the less expensive one. He said, "Some people need to pay more." I have the impression that when Walter spoke, he was insightful and funny. My mother once told me that Maggie and Walter would occasionally burst into their favorite songs and harmonize, but he died before I could know them as a couple.

For entertainment around 1900, Walter built a raft for use in Dalton Dam where he and friends floated around with their older children. Maggie was fond of taking her three youngsters on the train that ran north of Santa Anita race track to watch Lucky Baldwin race his horses. She took them on wagon rides to Norwalk and neighboring towns and bought berries for them from Jennie Dougherty Knott whose son Walter started Knott's Berry Farm. His friend Mr. Boysen created the boysenberry by grafting together the bushes of three other berries: raspberries, blackberries, and loganberries.

In her oral history, Maggie says she "engineered" the dinner that was served on December 20, 1907, when the Pacific Electric interurban railroad was completed from Los Angeles to Glendora. A separate note in her daughter's memoirs also gives her credit for this event. A meal was served to all those who arrived in the first red car — among them Henry Huntington.[8] What Maggie meant by the word "engineered" isn't clear, but she may have suggested that the celebration start with a free meal. She and Walter would have been active in the local business group as owners of a grocery store, and her managerial skills were strong. She may have commandeered her friends to contribute their favorite dishes. No matter how she participated, I enjoy the idea of her orchestrating a meal that Henry Huntington ate, and I was pleased to find a copy of *Blue Boy* in the background of a computer-enlarged family picture, though I doubt that Huntington gave it to her. The painting was popular with Victorians.

Writer Scott Peck says in his book *Searching for Stones* that everything is overdetermined.[9] In other words, there are many reasons for major changes, though most of us prefer the simplicity of naming one cause. Maggie and Walter's family left Glendora for Santa Monica in 1910, and though Maggie said Glendorans thought they were going to hell — an interesting comment on beach town morality — they had several reasons to leave. Walter suffered from asthma; they thought it would be easier for him to breathe ocean air. In 1909 their home next door to the Glendora Christian Church on Wabash had burned down. Glendorans saved all but one box of pictures and moved the young family into the upstairs living quarters of the Land Office, so the family was already displaced.[10] And customers were buying groceries from the De Shields' store on credit. One of Maggie's jobs was to ride around Glendora on her horse Jake, in her new culotte creation, trying to settle up accounts with squatters. Years later, she was still indignant that people couldn't pay what they owed.

The De Shields never mentally left Glendora. Both Walter and Maggie were in their mid-thirties when they moved their children into a house on Rose Avenue in Santa Monica, only a block or so from the beach. Most of their relatives were still in Glendora. Though in failing health and in a wheelchair, Maggie's mother, Jennie Shepperd, visited Maggie often. Her sister Olive Kamphefner thought her daughter Ethel would benefit from extended stays at the beach with her cousin Frances. Family members visited back and forth for years, but Glendora was home.

Maggie De Shields in culottes on her horse Jake

Walter and Maggie De Shields with their three children, (l-r) Glen, Frances, and Robert

In 1921, Emma De Shields Inman, Walter's sister, suggested that the old-timers of the Azusa Valley meet once a year to renew their commitment to pioneer history. It was a way to gather family and friends together.

Maggie used to introduce me to one old-timer after another at the picnics. As a child, I was looking up at kindly men and women hovering over me. The names that remained with me are Preston, Dougherty, Odell, Whitcomb, Knott, even Dalton. Many appear in the picnic pictures in both the Azusa and Glendora museums. When I look at them now, I realize how important family was to Maggie. The children from other families seldom appear in the pictures, though they attended the picnics, but the De Shields family children sat or stood in the front row of each picture. Only Maggie included all her offspring and positioned herself, white-haired and stately, in the middle. For good reason. She was the one holding both our family and the pioneer group together.

Maggie's handwritten minutes of the pioneer meetings disappeared when she was moved to a convalescent home in 1970, and I contend she may have entrusted someone in the community with the ledgers. When the last volume was located, I was thrilled to see my great-grandmother's handwriting, then amazed at Irene Taylor's note about her in the 1970 minutes. Irene was Earl Whitcomb's wife and the secretary pro tem. She wrote that Maggie De Shields was missing her first meeting in forty-five years and sent her regrets. She added, "Her minutes

(L-r) Unidentified girl, Mary Margaret Shepperd, and sister Cora, c. 1890

John Casey's grandchildren: (l-r) Lorena Frances Casey, John Walter De Shields, and Mary Nixon Casey

are full of her personal humor and philosophy." The group agreed to send her a plant or flowers with a wish for her recovery and presence at the 1971 picnic.

She didn't recover, though. She was ninety-six in 1971. The minutes of that meeting read, "Glenn Odell reported that he had just received word that Mrs. Maggie De Shields, our beloved secretary and longtime member, had passed away just this morning." Her name appears at the end of the list of pioneers who died that year.

So many things about this short note move me. That she had lived long enough to unify the early pioneers and their descendants, that her

The Shepperds, Kamphefners, and De Shields family with tiny Blue Boy *on credenza, c. 1895*

friendships with Glenn Odell and all the other old-timers in the group lasted a lifetime, that she died on a day that meant so much to her, that she was valued and beloved. I have a memory of my grandmother on the phone with Glenn Odell on the morning of her death, but I may be remembering what my mother told me. And if I add to this the miracle that's guiding me to put together this book, so many years later, I can't help but feel awe and purpose.

Maggie De Shields gave much of herself to the preservation of Glendora's history. Her name appears over and over again in our local museums, and mementos of her family were buried under the rock in front of Azusa City Hall. I'm sharing a copy of her poem "The Real Folks" along with her recipe for corn cakes at the end of this chapter.

In 1973 when attrition ended the picnics, the pioneer group funds — $215.06 — were divided between the Glendora Historical Society, founded in 1947, and the Azusa Historical Society, incorporated in 1964. Other local towns also formed historical groups. For a while, participation in the picnic and town groups overlapped. All members shared a desire to honor and record the past, but as time went on, the history of the land was separated from its earliest role as part of the Azusa Rancho. Memorabilia found its way into one museum or another,

Seated (l-r): Robert W. De Shields, June Duff, Jean Bacchilega, Billie De Shields, and Glen De Shields. Standing (l-r): Frances Rae Patten, Jim Duff, Frances Patten, and Walter and Maggie De Shields, 1942.

and so, the accompanying stories were divided up with it.

Something else happened two months after the last picnic in 1973 that should have ensured our understanding of local history. One member of the Memorial Day group, Violet Millar, gave a set of reel-to-reel tapes to the Glendora museum. She was Donell Spencer's daughter, and he was a local historian who served as president of both the Glendora and Azusa museums. He was the one who recorded the tapes that were made at the picnics. The Glendora Historical Society had also recorded some of the verbal histories, and some were labelled inadequately so that it's impossible to identify the occasions, locales, and dates of the tapings. But all of them are part of an oral history of the valley, and all of them disappeared. When I started working in the Glendora museum, no one knew anything about the tapes. Nor did I. I had only a vague memory of speakers at a podium in the Azusa auditorium on Memorial Day while someone played with a microphone and box behind them.

In October 2006 while I was on vacation, a man called the museum to say his mother had died and he'd found a box of reel-to-reel tapes, labelled Glendora Historical Society (GHS). Georgia Hawthorne, the curator at that time, asked him to read some of the names on the labels. She recognized De Shields from my quest to trace my family history and told him GHS would pay the postage to have them returned. My guess is that his mother took the tapes home for safekeeping and forgot to return them — for thirty-three years.

I knew what the tapes were the minute I saw them. They were interviews of the old-timers who shared their stories each year at the picnics. They were also my means of completing the task my great-grandmother had set for herself to preserve local history. John Lundstrom, then President of the Glendora Historical Society, supported my project to have the contents of the tapes moved to CDs, and today you can listen to them in the Azusa and Glendora museums, the Citrus College Library, or the Azusa Pacific University, Special Collections Library. The speakers on the tapes knew they'd made history, and they wanted all of us to hear their stories.

Aunt Maggie's 1895 Corn Cakes

Beat to blend---------------------------1 egg
Add condensed milk------------------½ cup
water-------------------------------------½ cup
melted shortening, bacon
fryings preferred-----------------------2 table spoons

Measure sifted flour-------------------1 cup
Yellow corn meal ----------------------1 1/4 cup
Baking powder-------------------------3 tea spoons
Sugar-------------------------------------2 table spoons

Put last four ingredients in sifter and sift into egg and milk mixture. Mix well and drop by spoon fulls into well greased heavy skillet. Cover and cook about 5 minutes on each side, over low flame. Do not rush cooking as the cakes are quite thick.

These make a nice lunch split and buttered with syrup if desired, or with a green vegetable, a wiener or slice of cold meat. You might try this: drop a portion of the mixture in skillet, place a wiener on it, then put more mixture on top of the wiener - when cooked you have a fine hot sandwich.

The Real Folks
by Maggie De Shields
May 30, 1925

I wish to say no harm, folks,
Against your time and mine -
Nor even of the younger folks
As we drift along with time.
But of the old timers of this valley
There are things I'd like to say
For the old time folks were the real folks
In the good old fashioned way.

They lived on ranches far apart.
And had they railroads? No!
Nor even yet a streetcar
To take them to and fro.
But if a neighbor needed help
Or in a sick bed lay,
The old time folks were the real folks
In the good old fashioned way.

'Twas not an automobile
That took them here and yon
To tell them of some needed help
For Charley, Bill or John.
But could we turn aback and look
Without a thought to lag -
Methinks we'd see them jogging 'long
'Hind some old faithful nag.
And in event that faithful nag
Had other work in trust
I'm sure we'd see "shanks horses"
'A-plodding through the dust.

I really believe those old times
Were happier than today
For the good old time folks were the real folks
In the good old fashioned way.

When neighbor went to neighbor
And asked a little aid,
Think an excuse they tried to give
For fear they'd not be paid?
Think you we'd hear them say these words?
"I'm sorry folks for you -
But I've a Mahjong party, or
I play bridge at two."
Don't really mean to criticize
The people of today
But the old time folks were the real folks
In the good old fashioned way.

The news - they didn't find it out
By telephone, we know.
Ten minute calls were not their style -
Perhaps a dress to show.
And when their visiting they did
And walked from home to home,
Think you they called some helper in
Or left their kids alone?
Where mother went, her children went,
Left early and stayed all day.
For the old time folks were the real folks
In the good old fashioned way.

I believe they were a peaceful sort.
No quarrels would they start.
They lived like one big family
Tho they lived miles apart.
They were God-fearing, I am sure,
And meant to do the right.
They tried to live the Golden Rule.
They didn't want to fight.

But if outsiders interfered
As I have heard them tell -
They'd cast religion to one side,
And folks, they'd fight like - Well,
They had to do that very thing
For water rights they say -
And the old time folks were the real folks
In the good old fashioned way.

An adobe hut was their first school
That's what I've heard them tell.
Say, can't you almost hear the ring
Of that old brass hand bell?
And can't you see those youngsters run
And gather without fail
'Round that old stump that held for them
The old tin water pail?
And can't you see that water drip
As those kids raised it up
In that old gourd, that was for them
An A-1 drinking cup?
Their second school, a grand affair-
Five hundred dollars, men! -
Meant weary toil and sacrifice
For all those farmers then.
It showed their sense of enterprise
Was much, friends, in their day
But the old time folks were the real folks
In the good old fashioned way.

Now our lives, they may seem to be
Important, 'twas ever thus,
But could we, would we, stand today
What those folks stood for us?
At any rate I feel like this
Tho I do the best I can,
Whene'er I see those old time folks
I wish I were a man

That I might tip my hat to them,
A reverence reveal,
For all the hardships they endured.
Folks, that is how I feel.
So when the old year rolls around
Let's pledge here at this rally
To do the best for those who're left
The old timers of this valley.
They lived a good and simple life
In a good and glorious day
For the old time folks were the real folks
In the good old fashioned way.

The Cullen Legacy

Bill Cullen II, December 2007

Bill Cullen II was a man of ideas. Though his body wasn't keeping up with his lively spirit in 2008 when I interviewed him, one thing made his eyes sparkle — the thought that he'd grown up along with the city of Glendora. Much of its growth has been the result of his *finagling*, a word he used often when he referred to his career. It meant he brought together developers and financiers, or laid out tracts of land, or negotiated with the city council. When asked, he said he'd been a consultant and a realtor. Though the scope of his own accomplishments amazed him, Glendorans have been the ones who benefitted from most of his plans. They've provided jobs and housing and perks that all of us take for granted.

Among Cullen's many projects were the Glendora Country Club, the Foothill Presbyterian Hospital, the Glenoaks Golf Course, the west side of Valley Center, and housing tracts: the Cullen Ranch, Hidden Springs, and Oak Tree Rancho. Even the width of Lone Hill Avenue was the result of Cullen's foresight. It was designed to be only sixty feet wide, but he anticipated traffic growth and, as a board member on the Planning Commission, suggested more width. Thank goodness.

Bill Cullen was born in 1921 when the city was citrus groves. His specialty was land usage at a time when there was plenty of land to use. He wasn't a developer and criticized them for having little patience, but he knew how to work with them and with the city government to nurture land developments to completion.

His potential as a community leader was recognized early. He was student body president of Citrus High School and continued his leadership role at Citrus Jr. College. He met his wife, Marion Edith Crain, in about 1938 when his mother heard her brother George, a minister, speak at a Christian convention in Long Beach and invited him to speak at the Glendora church. Bill and Marion married in 1941 and had four children: Pam, Karen, Bill III, and John. Today Pam Rodewald is a retired sixth grade teacher living in San Luis Obispo. Karen lives with her husband Dan Wilshire in the home that her great-grandfather built. She taught elementary school for thirty-four years in the Glendora Unified School District, and the couple spent seventeen years running a youth orchestra at Citrus College. William has passed away, and John retired to Mexico after a career teaching science at Glendora High School.

The Cullens have always been citrus growers, so Bill grew up knowing about the care of oranges. One of his first jobs was picking early off-bloom navel oranges on a neighbor's property that he sold for fifty cents for a fifty-pound box. He figured he earned about thirty-five cents an hour. He took care of many groves in the area, including his own family's, but eventually found his way to more creative endeavors.

Karen Cullen and Dan Wilshire

The Cullen Ranch was his first land development project in 1961. Bill and his brother-in-law, Paul Roll, completed the plans for the construction of about thirty homes on the family ranch bordered by Leadora on the south, Cullen on the west, Live Oak on the east, and Virginia on the north. Harold Herscher was the contractor, with the Leonard O. Ray Company as sales agents. At the time, the homes were touted as combining the old with the new for "gracious California living" and included all electric kitchens. This project was the first of a series of housing tracts that Cullen created to his own high standards.

Working again with Leonard Ray, Harold Herscher, and this time with Bill Bird of Ray Bird & Associates, he created Hidden Springs, a development north of Sierra Madre. The expansive one-story homes have garages that do not face the street. Each lot is large enough for driveways, swimming pools, and other features that homeowners want in their yards, and Cullen wrote the descriptions of them himself. The homes sold for about $35,000, a significant price then. In another project, Cullen helped a developer lay out the streets of Oak Tree Rancho to avoid the oak trees. Now camellias proliferate in the shade of the trees, and the curving streets just north of the high school suggest a genteel lifestyle.

The eighty or ninety acres of the Glendora Country Club once belonged to the Warren Ranch, and the clubhouse used to be Bill Warren's family home. Bill Cullen remembers high school parties on the ranch. Mr. Casper, a neighbor, used to play the piano and sing so Cullen and his classmates could dance. One day, Bill Cullen and another Allandale realtor, named Warren Beach, started talking about golf courses, and Bill suggested a golf course for Glendora. They toured the property. Bill spoke to Les Warren about selling the ranch and confirmed that a stream ran through it. (Foothill Boulevard was constructed around the land because it was swampy.) Les and Bill were willing to sell their property which was county, not city, land. Soon there was enough interest to build the club. Bill laid out both the golf course and the one row of lots for houses to border it, so the proceeds from those homes financed the first nine holes east of Amelia. The Rain Bird Company was hired to engineer the sprinklers for the entire golf course after Cullen and Warren Beach determined the length of each hole.

The second nine holes were problematic because the aqueduct runs across the property west of Amelia, as does a drainage creek. It was difficult to grade the land, and Bill had to figure out how to tap into the water, supplied to the Warren Ranch by the Glendora Irrigating Company. At that time, permits weren't required, so Bill and his team dug across Amelia Avenue to put a water pipe through to the second nine holes. He and Warren Beach went on to build the Glenoaks Golf Course that Bill named by combining Charter Oaks with Glendora. Later they created a third pitch and putt in Anaheim and a fourth course east of Ontario.

To build something that makes money and creates jobs was satisfying for Bill Cullen, and he chuckled over his ability to do that. He knew Glendora land. He knew where ditches, trenches, concrete walls, and pipelines cross properties. When he spoke of a piece of land, he talked about its history. *Zanjeros*, ditch riders, used to travel horseback along the ditch where the Covina pipeline runs through Glenoaks Golf Course today. In the 1870s, these men were paid to regulate the flow of water. They opened and closed irrigation feeds at certain times of the day or cleaned out debris that would stop or change the flow of water. They were paid to do so. The *zanjeros* were probably armed because the early settlers went to the ditch with pistols, though no one used them. Both ranchero Dalton and the settlers had been known to divert the flow of water to their own thirsty fields, and squatters and vagrants would often help themselves to water that was already in short supply. They were all ready to fight. Regulation was meant to keep water usage equitable. In about 1885, Christians held baptisms where the ditch crossed what are now Citrus and Foothill Boulevards. But Bill's grandmother, Mary Alice Fitzgerald, didn't participate because she was an Irish Catholic, Bill added. He had a subtle sense of humor.

His later projects were more ambitious. In 1965, Bill "planted the seed" for the Foothill Presbyterian Hospital in a conversation with C.M. Johnston at a board meeting of the Glendora Citrus Association. Johnston said he wanted to donate land to create a memorial for his late and only son, Dr. Morris Lee Johnston. Bill suggested a hospital, then spoke with Leonard Ray who, in turn, went to his Presbyterian Church for support. The city of Glendora later enabled the sale of tax-exempt bonds in 1970, so the hospital became a reality.

When Everett Hughes bought property on the west side of Valley Center Avenue in about 1975, he hired Cullen to work full-time on the project with him.

No one can predict the impact of his own work on a community. A spoken idea can extend itself across both land and time. In Bill Cullen's case, his dedication to the well-being of Glendorans extends back two additional generations.

John Walter Cullen and May Engelhardt were Bill's parents. Both of them were children of original pioneer families. Their home was located at 554 N. Cullen Ave., but the original house has been rebuilt. They owned both orange and lemon groves and were involved in the citrus industry. They were also active in the Christian Church, paying the reverend when no one had any money. They had four children: John, Richard, Catherine, and Bill (William Bryant II). Both parents were as spirited as their offspring.

John Walter inherited his interest in gold from his father who had a gold mine in the foothills and used to bring down ore for the assay work that John Walter continued to do in his garage after his father's passing. Assay work requires weights and machinery that would separate the ore from the dirt around it. And as an elder in the First Christian Church, he helped in the construction of the current building on Bennett and Glendora Avenues.

May's parents were also active in the church and met with other Christians in a grove west of Citrus College by the old Azusa ditch on Casey land to worship. They were charter members of that church in 1885. May herself traveled to the Big Island of Hawaii in 1902 where she was a Christian missionary in Hilo for a couple of years. She worked in both a school and a hospital there, and later attended the Good Samaritan School of Nursing, becoming a registered nurse in 1908. She married John Walter in 1910. He passed away in 1951, and she eventually died at the age of ninety-two in 1970. Catherine Roll, Bill's sister, was a hundred years old when she died in 2015 in Yucca Valley.

When asked about his family, Bill talked about the loss of his older brothers, both at a young age and both in the foothills of Glendora. His brother Jack died at about eighteen in 1928 at the mouth of the San Gabriel Canyon where he was supervising younger boys in the YMCA. They were playing running games like capture the flag when Jack tripped, fell into the creek, and broke his neck. His brother Richard was killed in a car accident on the way to El Encanto restaurant with a relative in 1940. The road was new, and a stranger ran through a stop sign at the curve where Azusa Avenue goes into the canyon.

Going back one more generation, Bill was quick to admit his grandfather wasn't the first Glendora citizen that he's reputed to be and chuckles when he adds that Glendora didn't exist when his ancestors got here. He's right. His grandfather's influence was felt long before the Glendora dream.

William Bryant Cullen I was born in 1841 in Virginia to John Brennon Cullen, a dentist, and Harriet Furr. The Furr family was closely connected to George Washington's mother whose last name was Ball, so the Cullen history dates back to the beginning of the United States. The only picture of John Brennon is an oil painting done by his son who painted his father on the lid of a cigar box. Karen Cullen treasures that family heirloom in her home today.

William Bryant was attending the University of Mississippi when Virginia started organizing volunteers for the Confederate Army in 1861. He joined the Lamar Rifles, a group assigned to the Virginia army, and so, participated in the first battles of the war: Manassas, Yorktown, Williamsburg, West Point, and Seven Pines or Fair Oaks. He lost an arm in the latter battle, so he spent the rest of the war as a dispatch officer taking messages from one general to another.

William Bryant Cullen
with one arm, 1862

John Brennon Cullen sans forceps,
c. 1870

After the war, he turned to mercantile and government work in Memphis, Tennessee, and was active in the Cotton Compress Association. He was also the license collector for the city of Memphis for several years. There, he met and married Mary Alice Fitzgerald in 1870.

Mary's father had brought his child to Memphis from Youghal, Ireland, after her mother died. But her father also passed away, so Mary was raised in a convent. Two of Mary and William Bryant's eight children were born in Memphis — Mary Maud and John Walter — and another six were born in California. They were Etta, Margaret, Clara, William Gerald, Agnes, and Edward Owen. Maud never married. Etta's married name was Reynard; Clara married John Rieker. Margaret married Bert Roll, and Agnes married Engbert Van der Sluis. Gerald married Sue Nichols Sutherland. Owen was killed in a mining accident in northern California.

Luck brought the Cullens to California in 1874. The postwar economy and a yellow fever epidemic in the South made the West sound idyllic. William Bryant wanted to move his young family to Texas, but John Bender, his boyhood friend and business partner, wanted to move to California. They flipped a coin, and Cullen lost the toss. To this day, the Cullen family applauds both Bender's good sense and his win.

It wasn't easy to reach Los Angeles. With their two small children and John Bender, the Cullens took the new transcontinental railway from Omaha to San Francisco, then traveled by ship to San Pedro, and by wagon or stagecoach to Los Angeles. By the end of the year, Bender and

LEFT: *William Bryant Cullen, c. 1880*

RIGHT: *Nellie May Engelhardt Cullen, the Christian missionary to Hawaii, c. 1902*

LEFT MIDDLE: *The Cullen women (l-r): Clara, Maud, Agnes, Margaret, Etta, c. 1890*

The Cullen Family in 1892 with Mary Alice Fitzgerald and William Bryant Cullen, seated left and right

Cullen had both found their way to the disputed land of the Azusa Valley.

Envision sky and land and mountains. There were sycamores and oaks. Scattered farmhouses and barns stood miles apart. Miners and Indians wandered the foothills, and there were few fences. The city of Glendora did not exist when Bender and Cullen arrived. Nor did Azusa. But the fight between Dalton and the homesteaders was well underway, and it was as complicated as a land dispute can be.

An astoundingly brief summary: Henry Dalton, a British merchant, purchased Mexican land grants to the Rancho Azusa and part of the Rancho San José in 1844. When California became a state in 1850, the land that is now Glendora was part of Henry Dalton's Rancho Azusa. The Land Act of 1851 questioned the validity and boundaries of Spanish and Mexican land grants throughout the state, despite the government's agreement with Mexico to honor those claims. California was in transition, and Dalton was caught in the middle of it. He hired men to survey his vast holdings, though land measurements themselves were often inaccurate.

Whether he was right or wrong, a government surveyor told settlers that Dalton did not own the land between about Citrus Avenue and the west side of San Dimas and that they should file claims on it or others would. The legal battle began. The courts heard litigation over the disputed land for about twenty-nine years — until a federal court ruled in 1881 in favor of the homesteaders. By that time, some of them had been living on their claims for over twenty years, and Dalton was old and penniless.

Cullen and Bender must have heard about the dispute when they arrived in Alhambra and then Duarte in 1874. They lived briefly in each township before they found open land in the Azusa Valley. Bender claimed 160 acres just west of what is now Glendora Avenue and north of the current Foothill Boulevard. He bought some of this land from Wolf and Barnes, two early settlers who apparently decided not to cultivate the land for five years as required by the Homestead Act of 1862.

Cullen's acreage included the land that became the original town of Glendora. His claim is now bordered approximately by Sierra Madre, Glendora (Michigan), Meda or Bennett, and Live Oak Avenues. He purchased the right to the land from John Gassaway with no guarantee that he'd eventually own it. Dalton's claim to it was making its way to the Supreme Court, and Cullen would have known, too, that the Homestead Act excluded men who had borne arms against the United States. As a Confederate soldier, William Bryant I had done just that. But so had Dalton. Dalton had married into a Mexican family and appeared to have sided with Mexico during the Mexican-American War.

William Bryant was taking no chances. He had a family to raise, so they lived in a woodcutter's shack with a dirt floor on his property while

The Cullen Family, c. 1895

he waited in hopes that the court would give him the title to his land. He searched the area for springs and filed additional land claims on the two he found. The main one was on the east side of the valley on the hill going up to what is now Bluebird Ranch. The hardship of living on barren land proved too much for many an early settler, but Cullen did what he could with only one arm. William Bryant hired someone to dig a well twenty or thirty feet deep on his property in hopes of finding water. He didn't find any, and the well became an outhouse. When inside facilities later became fashionable, Mary Alice objected to having a privy in the house, but her husband won the argument.

The Cullens' first water supply came through molded concrete pipe from Engelhardt (now Englewild) Canyon. William Bryant hired a man who owned a device that would make a seamless pipe of cement as it moved along a ditch. He and Bender also worked to bring water down from the Dalton canyons in reamed-out bamboo pipes. Bamboo still grows in the foothills as a result of their work.

Despite his handicap, William Bryant cleared the land and planted castor beans, whose oil was used to lubricate wagon wheels. He also planted twenty to forty acres of grapes and had a winery and a garden. Surely his wife Mary Alice helped with all this, in addition to raising eight children. In pictures, she appears to be a robust and good-natured helpmate.

William Bryant could extract teeth, too. When he left Memphis for California, his father equipped him with a pair of forceps in case he wanted to pursue that line of work. He did pull an occasional tooth, and once he was elected justice of the peace in 1876, he also performed

John Walter and May Engelhardt Cullen

marriages. But money was scarce. William Bryant spent 1879 to 1882 as the County Tax Collector in Los Angeles — a job well suited for a man wielding forceps. The deputy tax collector under him was A.E. Sepulveda, and the tax on 160 acres was eight dollars. He returned to the Azusa Valley only after he had clear title to his property.

The first Cullen house was built in 1880 with wood from Eldoradoville in the San Gabriel foothills, but that home on Cullen Avenue has been rebuilt. When he married in 1910, William's son John Walter built a house where Virginia deadends into Cullen Avenue. It was north of the original ranch house. The home on the corner of Virginia and Minnesota Avenues, where Karen Cullen and Dan Wilshire currently live, was built on Cullen land in 1890 by Henry D. Engelhardt and his wife Katherine Kamphefner, Karen's maternal great-grandparents. They bought the land from William Bryant, and Engelhardts have lived there ever since.

William Bryant Cullen I is known as the first postmaster of Glendora, but the city did not exist when he started his new position in the Alosta post office — his home. The entire area, including Glendora, Azusa, and Covina, was known as the Azusa Valley in the early 1880s. It remained the Azusa Valley until Harrison Fuller bought the original Barnes property from W.H. Potts and petitioned Washington for a post office. On the pioneer map, his land is just west of Glendora Avenue and between the Cullen and Bender claims. To name a post office is to name a locality, so Fuller named it after his daughter Anna Losta: Alosta. Thus, the name preceded that of Glendora and was used informally by residents living near the post office. For several years, it was located in Cullen's home, and the mail was sorted in a J. & P. Coats thread box. That box is in the historical museum today.

Lots were first sold in the city of Glendora on April 1, 1887. In July of that year, Dr. A.E. Engelhardt was appointed postmaster, and the mail was moved from the Cullen home to the store that he ran with his brother John on the northeast corner of Whitcomb and Vista Bonita Avenues. Then on March 22, 1888, the Glendora *Signal* reported that Dr. August E. Engelhardt had received his commission as postmaster from Washington. So although Cullen served several years as the Alosta postmaster, he worked only two or three months as postmaster for Glendora. (The Alosta

Bill and Marion Cullen with daughter Karen

post office was reestablished in 1888 one mile south of Glendora, but it was discontinued in 1899.)

William Bryant also wired local ranches for the Morse code before the Santa Fe Railway came through Glendora in 1887. Once that happened, he intercepted the news at the railroad station and shared it with the community. One Glendoran, Carol Treacy, remembers how exciting it was to watch a man tap out a telegram at the railroad station as late as the 1940s.

To look at the Cullen family tree is to understand how close the original pioneers of the valley were. They married into each other's families. Here's a brief sample from the Cullen genealogy: Katherine Kamphefner married Henry Engelhardt. May Engelhardt married Walter Cullen. Rosa Engelhardt married Thomas Kamphefner. There were double cousins in these families, and because Thomas Kamphefner's brother Henry was married to Olive Shepperd, I am related to them, too. My great-grandmother Maggie Shepperd De Shields was Olive Shepperd Kamphefner's sister. Are you following this? Bill Cullen told me that he spent a lot of time as a child at Henry and Olive Kamphefner's home in Little Dalton Canyon where the debris basin is now. They were his relatives, and the thought makes me happy.

It's a gift to share ancestors, and it's a fine thing, too, to find joy in your own work. Bill Cullen radiated the satisfaction of a life well lived until the day he died in June 2010 at eighty-nine years old. He remembered childhood games under citrus trees and picnics in Dalton Canyon, and his voice was joyful as he spoke of Glendora's beauty. The only parental caution he mentioned was that he wasn't to pick oranges in anyone else's orchard.

From the Civil War to Glendora
The Shepperd Family

Jennie Porter Collins, 1841-1919

Jacob Russell Shepperd, 1836-1920

If you enjoy wandering the old headstones in Oakdale Memorial Park, you may wonder who the Shepperds were and what they meant to Glendora. You already know three of the Shepperd daughters by other names: Whitcomb, Kamphefner, and De Shields. As in-laws of George Dexter and Leadora Whitcomb, the family lived at the center of town when the streets were being named in 1887, their daughter Meda inspiring the name of one of them, and their lives touched those of other Glendorans who also traveled west after the Civil War.

Like their neighbors, Jennie and Jacob were already part of the history of this country. They'd settled Indian territory, supported the Underground Railroad, suffered the repeal of the Missouri Compromise, and survived the war. Even their journey west on the new Santa Fe railroad from Kansas to Glendora in 1887 made them part of a larger tale. None of us can escape the events of our own time, but the growth of the country once seemed dependent on the well-being of Kansas, the place the Shepperds called home for more than thirty years. Their pioneer strength was born on the territorial plains outside Topeka and exemplifies the resilient spirit that once prompted Azusa Valley settlers to travel west to live in Whitcomb's new town.

Something about researching the family makes me want to sit down with Jennie and Jacob on their porch to chat about life in Kansas. They would have had a porch on the farmhouse overlooking their property, and their conversation would be rich with pioneer lore. Or we could talk over a meal of biscuits and gravy or corn in any of its numerous forms: bread, grits, mush, pudding, or pancakes. I can guarantee Jennie Shepperd knew how to cook them all. I'd love to ride out with her siblings or children to watch the herds of buffalo or to make trades with local Indians, even the ones that startled settlers by appearing in cabins to sample whatever the next meal would be.

Of course, I'm a fair-weather time-traveler. I'd happily forego the drought of 1860 or the Indian attacks of the 1860s and '70s, and I cower at the thought of the grasshopper onslaught of 1874 that leveled rich crops and left the water polluted with grasshopper poop and everything smelling of dead insects. More than anything else, I'd skip the bloodshed of the Civil War.

The story of the Shepperd family is worth adding to the history of Glendora because both the Union and the Confederacy were once well represented in the San Gabriel Valley, and Jacob found friends among Glendora's veterans.

His family lineage tells the story of the country. His great-great-grandparents lived in North Muskham, Nottinghamshire, England, in the early 1700s. His great-grandfather arrived in the United States in time for the Revolutionary War. He married a native of Virginia and fathered a son born in that state on July 4, 1776, the day we celebrate the signing of the Declaration of Independence. Jacob's father William was also a Virginia native and lived there until he and his wife Nancy moved to Illinois in the early 1830s. Jacob, their seventh child, was born there in 1836.

By the time he was twenty-three, Jacob had become a farmer and miller by trade, with personal property worth fifty dollars, according to the 1860 federal census. He lived with his father and his father's third wife, and a combination of eight Miller and Shepard (one of its many spellings) siblings on the family farm in Pleasant Grove, Des Moines, Iowa. The farm was valued at $3,500. Jacob was helping his father run the farm when he met Jennie Porter Collins and decided to marry her.

By that time, Jennie had lived in Kansas for about ten years. She was born in Ohio in 1841 and lost both parents as a child. Her mother died when she was six, and her father, Jacob Collins, a Methodist minister "of the old school" according to her obituary, died when his daughter was eleven. Her older siblings took Jennie to Kansas Territory in 1855, only a year after Indians agreed that the land could be opened to settlers.

The events of 1854 had many repercussions in United States history, and the Collins children were affected by all of them. In that year, Nebraska and Kansas settlers requested territorial status. The request reopened the contentious issue of slavery in Congress. Were new territories to be admitted as slave or free lands? The Kansas-Nebraska Act was passed, giving both territories the right to choose for themselves. Though this sounds reasonable out of context, the Act repealed the Missouri Compromise, an agreement that had guaranteed freedom for slaves in the new territories. Pro-slavery states were satisfied that Kansas would vote to determine its fate, and Nebraska was already committed to the Union. But the North was outraged enough to form a new party to replace the Whigs and to focus on antislavery as an issue. That year saw both the birth of the Republican Party and the renewal of Lincoln's political commitments, according to Doris Kearns Goodwin's *A Team of Rivals*.

The Kansas-Nebraska Act also meant that Kansas was to engage in an informal and local war fought neighbor-against-neighbor until the Civil War started officially in 1861 because settlers on both sides of the issue rushed west to influence votes. While the other states participated in a war that lasted about four years, Kansans suffered political violence for at least a decade.

No one in the family knows what prompted the Collins children to move to Kansas, but they may have had to move out of a parsonage after their minister father died. Perhaps an older brother had an adventurous streak, or they may have had relatives in the new territory. Even so, housing in Kansas was problematic when the land was first opened for settlement. There was nothing there but two or three trails and an occasional trading post. In her book, *Pioneer Women: Voices from the Kansas Frontier*, Joanna L. Stratton discusses the settlers' building options. On the eastern side of Kansas, timber and stone were plentiful, so homesteaders could build sturdy cabins. But on the west side of the state where the terrain was flat and vegetation sparse, settlers were forced to build sod huts out of the land itself or burrow into dugouts about fourteen square feet in diameter.

Life on the prairie engendered a type of camaraderie that became part of the pioneer character. Settlers often had to depend on the generosity of the families who preceded them for necessities. For example, Kansas winds could make it impossible to cook on an open fire outside a covered wagon, so women relied on the good will of those who had stoves inside cabins or dugouts. Water was scarce. Occasionally settlers traveled long distances to find town pumps locked, and so, had to find assistance. Water witching was a science. In the search for a desirable homestead, newcomers would request the aid of local dowsers who knew the skill of holding the forked branch of a peach or willow tree and walking back and forth over the land until the main stem of the rod bent toward the ground. Once this happened, someone had to dig down to the water table, in one case, sixty-five feet down. The Shepperds' eldest son, William Russell, learned this skill as he was growing up in Kansas and gained some notoriety for it later in the San Gabriel Valley.

While land was the goal of most northern settlers in Kansas during the mid-1850s, pro-slavery Missourians had other ideas. The term "bleeding Kansas" was coined to describe the violence between 1854 when the land was opened and 1861 when Kansas was admitted to the Union as a free state and Lincoln took office. Jennie Collins and her siblings would have been aware of political savagery. Her obituary says she had "all the experiences of the western frontier of that period, while wild buffalo and wild Indians ranged the plains." Eastern Kansas Indians were generally peaceful, but white pro-slavery activists in Missouri would cross the river into Kansas to stuff ballot boxes and influence elections, sometimes at gunpoint. Voter fraud was rampant, and retaliation was equally vicious. By March 19, 1856, the House of Representatives was investigating the violence between Kansas Territory and Missouri.

On May 24 and 25 of that year, John Brown decided to avenge the political aggressions of his pro-slavery neighbors. He was the captain of an emergency force recruited by abolitionists in Lawrence to protect them against Missourian raids. Living in Osawatomie, only about sixty miles from Lawrence and another twenty-seven from Topeka, John Brown and a small party which included his sons raided pro-slavery cabins on Pottawatomie Creek and murdered five men who were active in a local pro-slavery district court. News like this would have reached the Collins family. They were Union sympathizers and would have feared reprisal from pro-slavery activists. At that time, the territory was plagued with small bands of violent marauders who searched cabin to cabin for their political opponents. In the decade that Jennie lived in Kansas before she married, she and her siblings would have been aware of, if not involved in, this prelude to war. According to an inscription in a family Bible, the death of Jennie's twelve-year-old brother David Collins marked this period of time for her, though there's no indication of the cause of his death.

While the exact whereabouts of the Collins children between 1855 and 1861 is not known, most settlements were located in the eastern quarter of the territory then. The siblings were probably near Topeka where Jennie and Jacob settled after their marriage. If so, they were only a wagon ride from Lawrence or John Brown's settlement. Justice was slow to reach Brown after his raid. He fled the state and lived to commit another massacre at Harper's Ferry, Virginia, in 1859 and was hanged later that year. (His daughter traveled west with her family and is buried in Pasadena.)

Jennie's obituary says she united with the Christian Church at Des Moines, Iowa, when she was eighteen and "was baptized in the Des Moines river when the ice was a foot thick." A couple of 1861 addressed envelopes that have been passed down in my family suggest that both Jennie and Jacob spent part of that summer in Montezuma, Iowa, not far from Jacob's family home. Jennie may have been sent to visit relatives at the start of the war, so she and Jacob could have celebrated the beginning of Lincoln's presidency together or bemoaned the secession of the lower southern states.

The envelopes reflect the spirit of the time because both of them bear Union stamps. The Union flag adorns the left quarter of one of them. Its significance is increased when you know that Lincoln refused to remove the stars of those states that seceded as a result of his candidacy. The second envelope is more obviously pro-Union. It says UNION at the top of it, and the left quarter is stamped with a tree whose branches are individual union flags representing each state. Beneath the tree is this poem:

Traitor! spare that Tree,
Cleave not a single bough,
In youth it shelter'd me,
And I'll protect it now.

Civil War tree envelope

These are the first four lines of an 1837 poem by George Pope Morris. Only the first word was changed from "Woodman" to "Traitor!" for use on the Union postage stamp.

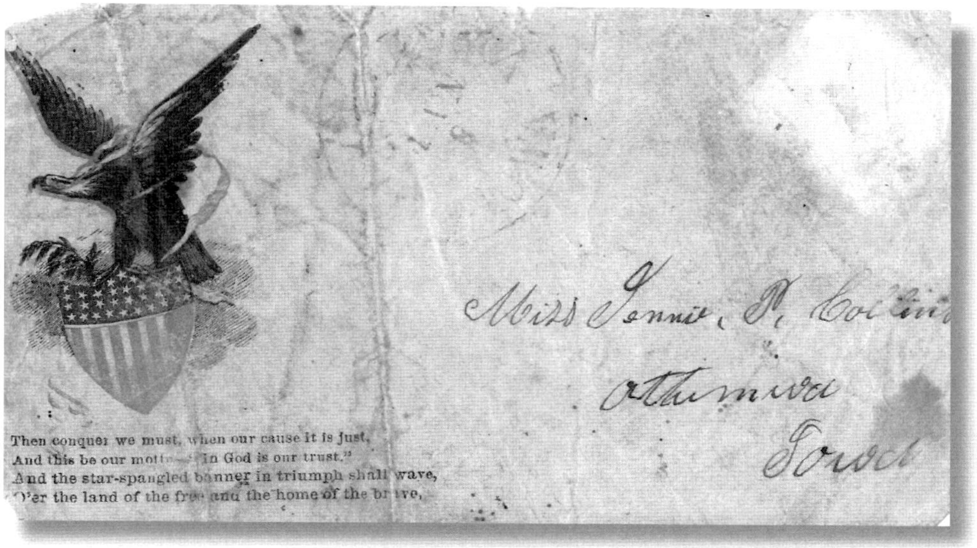

Civil War eagle envelope

Once they married in Burlington, Des Moines County, Iowa, on May 2, 1862, Jennie and Jacob settled in Topeka where they spent the war years. Their first child Letticia was born on February 19, 1863 and died three days later. They would still have been mourning her loss in August when Lawrence was attacked.

On Friday morning, August 21, 1863, a guerrilla band of over four hundred men from two counties in Missouri raided Lawrence, Kansas, under the command of William C. Quantrill. They crossed the river at night and rode about thirty miles westward, in the dark, to the hills above Lawrence so that the townspeople were still sleeping and unprotected when the attack began. Stories abound of the atrocities that were committed, and the result was the burning of about two hundred buildings and the deaths of about as many men.

Jacob was a member of the abolitionist Home Guard, a volunteer branch of the state militia in Topeka, and his service coincided with the raid on Lawrence. It's listed as the bloodiest battle of the Civil War fought on Kansas soil, but it wasn't a battle because the town wasn't armed. It was a massacre.

Topeka residents were horrified by the attack, and they feared for their own lives and property. The renegade troops had warned them that their town would be next. Only twenty-seven miles from Lawrence, about the distance from Glendora to Glendale, California, Topeka would have made a fine target for the raiders because it was the headquarters on the Lane Trail to Freedom on the National Underground Railroad. The Ritchie House still stands to commemorate the role Topeka played as one stop on the route to liberty.

Jacob Shepperd had duties as a member of the Home Guard. He may have been sent to Lawrence as part of a rescue team or to assist with burials. Some of the troops were sent east to participate in other states, but many remained as a defensive effort in Topeka. His assignment is unknown, but the raid took a toll on everyone living in that area.

One or two sentences in Jennie's obituary are missing where it's been torn. The part that remains hints at their suffering. It says that later their home was at Tecumseh, near Topeka "and she was personally. . . ." Something. The missing word remains a mystery. Then, for two years, she was the one responsible for the homestead and the family because Jacob was blind and ill of sunstroke. The lost sentences may have explained both Jacob's condition and their grief.

In Topeka on June 12, 1864, their son William Russell was born about ten months after Quantrill's raid and ten months before Lincoln's assassination. After the war, the family moved to southern Kansas, to Longton in Elk County, where their other children were born and raised and where Jennie became affiliated with the Baptist church.

Jennie's obituary says that the family traveled to Illinois and back in a covered wagon not long after the Civil War. During the five weeks they traveled eastward, "Mrs. Shepperd recovered her shattered health." They probably journeyed to Illinois to see Jacob's relatives and visit the farm near Decatur where he was raised. The young family would have needed nurturing, but the implausibility of recovering one's health on a wagon train underscores the psychological gulf between the 1870s and now.

Kansas census records confirm the Shepperds' residences almost every five years. The 1865 census places Jacob, Jennie, and their one son in Mission Creek, Wabaunsee County, Kansas, another town active in the Underground Railroad and near Topeka. In 1875, the Shepperd family consisted of five children, not counting the daughter lost in infancy, and they appear on the census that year in Longton, Howard County. In 1878, another child named Millie was born and died within a week, according to a family Bible. Then, the 1880 census finds the family in Labette, Kansas, with the six living children. The 1885 census places them back in Mission Creek with five of the six living children in the same residence.

Their eldest daughter Meda was living with her husband nearby. Meda Ella and George Bennett Whitcomb married in 1883 and appear on this census as a couple on a separate farm in Mission Creek. He was twenty-four and a farmer; she was nineteen. The young Whitcombs lived in Kansas for about three years before their son George Ernest was born and they moved to Glendora. Because Meda Ella and George Bennett were farming near her parents' homestead, it's easy to guess at the family dynamics that resulted in their move west.

George Bennett would have been anxious to join his parents in California. His father would have written enthusiastic letters about his plans for this new town, perhaps sharing the layout of the streets or his plans for the new Glendora Grammar school or the new depot, and his son probably missed the excitement of construction that was part of his father's life. The young man would have wanted to prove himself, too, because he was educated and had developed skills to rival his father's. He attended college sometime between 1880 when the census found him living in the family home in Chicago, Illinois, and the 1885 census showing him married and living with Meda in Kansas. He had Whitcomb blood and wouldn't have been contented to remain a Kansas farmer.

As a young husband, George Bennett would have been anxious to ingratiate himself with his wife's family, perhaps regaling them with stories of his father's business skills or bragging about his parents' successes. Perhaps he was silent and let Meda convince her parents that the Whitcombs would make the move to a new state easy. No one knows. But George Dexter and Leadora would certainly have written more often and entreated their son more fervently once they knew that Meda was pregnant with their first grandchild. Even if George Bennett wasn't susceptible to his parents' entreaties, he would have seen the advertisements touting California. He had his own dreams of new towns.

His wife could have posed a problem. Meda Ella wouldn't have wanted to sacrifice their farmland for a trek to California with a new baby. She needed her mother's and sisters' help and may have told George Bennett she wouldn't move without them. By 1886, Jennie and Jacob were about fifty years old and had improved their lives as much as they could in Kansas. Family pictures prove they had achieved a comfortable lifestyle. Their children were fashionable young adults posing for a professional photographer's camera. It's never easy to pull up stakes after a lifetime in one place, but the Shepperds knew their children would have more options in California. Their son-in-law would have assured them that his parents were influential and that they'd help make the transition easy for the family. The bottom line was that Jennie and Jacob didn't want to lose their oldest living daughter to California, and that was where she, George Bennett, and their new baby were going. So with caution, the Shepperds started planning the move.

William Russell did not move west with his birth family, though he later joined them and made Glendora his home for the rest of his life. When he was twenty-three and his family moved west, he married and went to live in Indian Territory that didn't become the state of Oklahoma until 1907. His marriage was brief, and court papers show it was annulled in 1891.

Meda Ella and George Bennett Whitcomb arrived in Glendora in 1886 about a year before her parents and their four other children, ages eight, twelve, fourteen and sixteen, boarded the train in Kansas. The young Whitcombs moved into a home next door to Dr. August and Rosa Engelhardt where they lived only three years before George Bennett whisked his young family, now including a second son Walter, to Oregon where they founded the town of Whitcomb. Dr. Engelhardt probably delivered Walter, as he did most of the Shepperd and Glendora babies.

The Shepperd family arrived in Glendora on December 2, 1887, according to daughter Maggie Shepperd De Shields who was taped as she spoke about her family years later at one of the picnics of the Old Settlers of the East San Gabriel Valley. Even as an elderly woman she was still talking about their arrival on one of the first trains to stop in Glendora. The novelty of train travel and interest in the Whitcomb family would have made the arrival of their in-laws something to witness.

Donald Pflueger writes in his book, *Glendora*, that the first Santa Fe train arrived on May 31, 1887. The Glendora *Signal* was printing train schedules before October 20 when the newspaper alerted citizens that the new depot would be ready for business by November 10. This means the arrival of trains predated the completion of the depot. A report in the same newspaper on Thursday, October 22 says, "Mr. J.R. Shepperd, of Kansas, is expected soon to start a restaurant in Glendora." The town was excited by arrivals and departures that connected Glendora to Los Angeles and eastern states. Their town was on the map, and citizens were in the mood to celebrate.

The Glendora restaurant opened in March 1888 as Jennie's venture. Her initials are those on the ads that appeared in the Glendora *Signal* on March 1 and 8 with a note that the restaurant was already doing a good business. Meals were twenty-five cents and a 21-meal deal could be had for a mere $4.50. Apparently her husband helped with the baking because Jacob claimed that occupation on a voter registration form. The restaurant was located behind Jeffrey's Dry Goods store on Wabash, a business that advertised in the 1900 Citrus High School annual. The main street was still Vista Bonita, and Dr. Engelhardt had just received his commission that month from Washington to serve as postmaster of the new Glendora post office located in the drugstore he ran with his brother. Prior to that, the post office (i.e., the thread box) had been called Alosta and was located in the Cullen house for about four years. Now the name Alosta could be used for the post office in the town that Major George E. Gard, a land speculator, had established about a mile south of Glendora.

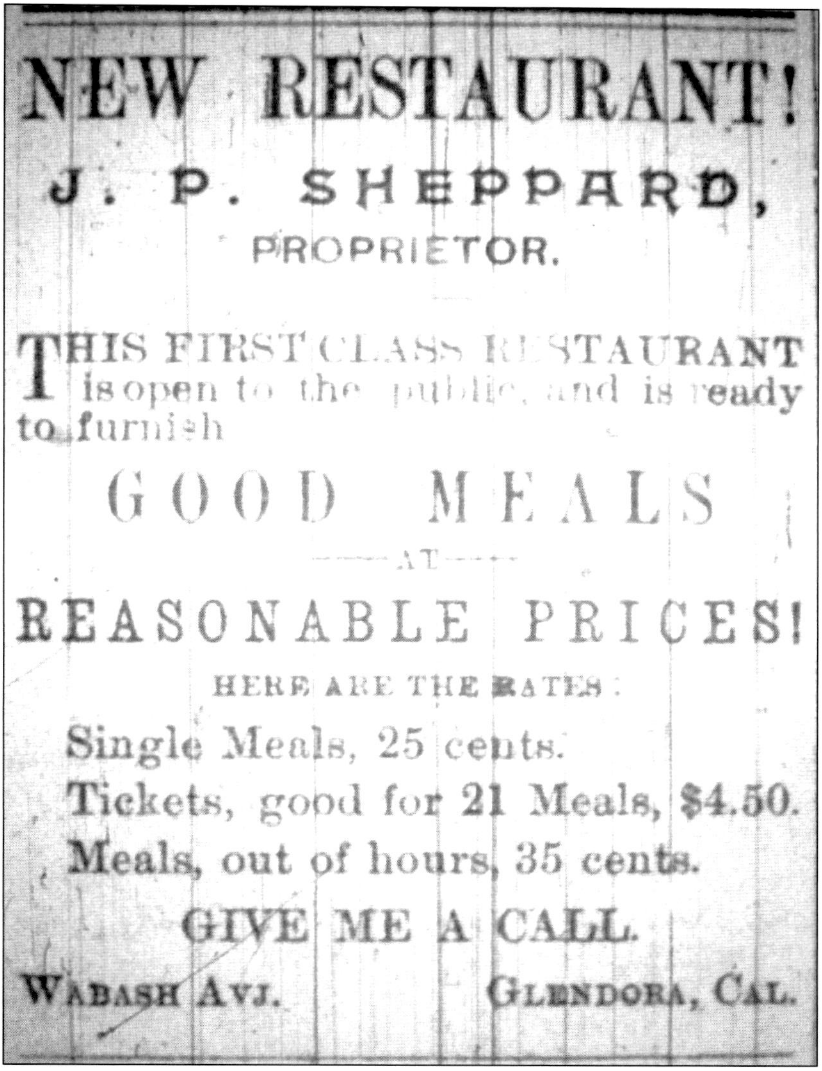
NEW RESTAURANT!
J. P. SHEPPARD,
PROPRIETOR.
THIS FIRST CLASS RESTAURANT is open to the public, and is ready to furnish
GOOD MEALS
AT
REASONABLE PRICES!
HERE ARE THE RATES:
Single Meals, 25 cents.
Tickets, good for 21 Meals, $4.50.
Meals, out of hours, 35 cents.
GIVE ME A CALL.
WABASH AVE.
GLENDORA, CAL.

Ad for the Glendora Restaurant in the Glendora Signal, *March 1888*

The Shepperds needed a home as well as an occupation, and the Whitcombs would have helped them find it. Maggie reported to the Glendora Women's Club in the 1940s that her parents had lived in the old Bradley house. That house may have been the predecessor of the Victorian home at 736 N. Vista Bonita Ave. The original home burned down in about 1910 and was rebuilt. Pictures of the Shepperd family home echo the style of the house that now stands there, and both have a front porch that forms an L around the right side. It was once the home of Ada Bradley and Carroll Whitcomb, but because the original home is gone, there's no way to prove it's the home in Shepperd photos.

Tintype of Jennie and Jacob Shepperd, c. 1890

Wherever the house stood, Jacob and Jennie had many pictures taken in front of it, but by 1900, they'd moved in with their daughter Olive, her husband Henry Kamphefner and their children in Little Dalton Canyon where they'd homesteaded 160 acres where the debris basin is now.

Glendora was once a small town. By 1900, the Shepperd girls had graduated from Glendora Grammar School and had married into local families. Maggie married Walter De Shields whose grandfather, John Casey, was the first filer for a homestead in the valley, and her sister Olive married Henry Kamphefner whose brother Thomas owned one of the local stores. Cora married Jim Campbell and moved to Los Angeles. The Shepperd brothers raised families and were active in the community for years. Frank Shepperd's name is first on the title deed of the house at 217 E. Leadora Ave. He broke horses and was a tunneler, a career required for both mining and civil engineering. Married twice, a family picture shows Frank and his second wife Addie posed on a motorcycle in an Azusa parade. When William Russell finally found his way to Glendora in 1910, he bought land on Route 66 where he built his house and planted a citrus orchard. The house was a car dealership in 2009 when I visited it with my relative Marquita Shepperd Barber who had grown up in the home.

According to family letters, Carroll Whitcomb stopped by the Shepperd home occasionally to hear news of his brother George Bennett and his family. Meda wrote her mother Jennie from Oregon, and the Whitcombs themselves went north to visit their eldest son and his wife on more than one occasion. After the Oregon couple lost three of four children to diphtheria and later divorced, Meda often returned for extended stays with her family in Glendora.

Jennie's activities appear in her obituary. She was active in the original Christian church on the northeast corner of Wabash and Bennett from 1888 until her death on April 18, 1919. It was the scene of many Shepperd events, including her own funeral service and her husband's. She was "an ardent worker in the cause of temperance and like reforms." She was active in the Good Templars, a British temperance group, and was "an honored member" of the Women's Christian Temperance Union. Abstinence was important to her and would have cemented her relationship with the Whitcombs.

Though the earliest settlers of the Azusa Valley did not travel east to fight in the Civil War, veterans on both sides of the slavery issue homesteaded here in the postwar years before Glendora was a town.

Evidence of the southern cause is easy to find in the museum. A picture of William Bryant Cullen commemorates his war injury. He lost an arm fighting in the battle of Seven Pines with the Confederate Army in Virginia. Later, he traveled west with his family to settle here in 1874. The United Daughters of the Confederacy existed as a women's group until about 1950, according to Donald Pflueger's book, *Glendora*, and the museum owns more than one of its scrapbooks.

Union veterans also opted to move west with their families. A Union soldier stands in uniform in the middle of the 1927 photograph of the old-timers of the East San Gabriel Valley, who met appropriately on Memorial Day every year for fifty years. On his hat are the letters GAR for Grand Army of the Republic. Glendora women formed the Ladies of the Grand Army of the Republic in 1908, and men had their own groups. George E. Gard, the founder of Alosta, was head of the Pacific Coast branches of the GAR in 1889, according to his biography.

John P. West, who was born in Ireland in 1825, was active in Iowa politics and fought in 1862 with the Fourteenth Regiment of the Iowa Volunteers. In 1872, he settled with his family in Compton, California. His sons, James L. and John Charles, bought over three hundred acres in the Azusa Township in 1878 and 1879. And the La Fetra brothers, Lawson and Milton, were abolitionists from Ohio who bought property, some of it Taggart land, here in 1883. Milton fought with the Ohio Volunteer Infantry against Early's Confederate forces in their raid on Washington.

George Dexter Whitcomb himself worked in Illinois for Union railroads during the Civil War, and Bartholomew Bradley, who owned the Glendora Livery Stable, enlisted in the Illinois Volunteer Infantry with his three brothers in 1862. Both men suffered losses in 1864 when the war ended. Bradley lost his wife and remarried a year later. George Dexter and Leadora lost an infant son in January of that year. It's impossible to know if shared grief, political sympathies, or mutual business skills formed the basis of the men's friendship, but the war experience

Shepperd, Kamphefner, and De Shields families in front of Shepperd home, c. 1910. Jennie, Jacob, and daughter Meda Shepperd are in the front row on the right.

Olive, Frank, and Maggie Shepperd in Topeka, Kansas, 1886

Frank and Addie Shepperd on a motorcycle in an Azusa parade, c. 1921

was common ground. Eventually, Bradley's daughter Ada married Whitcomb's son Carroll.

Jacob Shepperd's pallbearers were Dr. August Engelhardt, J.J. West, Frank Kaiser, and Charles La Fetra, noted in his obituary as old-timers and good friends since 1888. Women from the Gelwick, Bradley, Day, and Wilhite families sang hymns. Of those who participated in the service, the Bradley, La Fetra, and West families had all been Union supporters. Dr. Engelhardt was a child in Indiana during the Civil War.

TOP: *William Shepperd's home at 726 Route 66, c. 1910*

LEFT: *Frank Shepperd's home at 217 E. Leadora Ave., 2009*

Jacob's obituary says, "Death came as a relief from intense suffering." According to my grandmother, he became agitated in the late afternoon and would start walking. Concerned that he might get lost, I asked her how he got home. She said, "Oh, a neighbor would see him and bring him home in a wagon. Everyone knew him." The world was a different place when homesteads were miles apart and people had to rely on each other. I've seen more than one note on a family picture recording the exact age of its subject in more detail than we'd include today. Jacob's obituary states that he was "84 years, 1 month and 4 days old at the time of his death." Friends and neighbors in this valley shared a comfortable intimacy and an appreciation of the time they had together.

Jennie and Jacob Shepperd were active in the Glendora First Christian Church for more than thirty years when they passed away in 1919 and 1920, and they are buried alongside their daughter and her husband, Olive and Henry Kamphefner, and two of their three children, Ethel and Kenneth, my grandmother's cousins. Kenneth's death was as recent as 1990.

Whenever I wander the cemetery looking for the six generations of my family members who settled this town, I think of Emily Bronte's description of wandering amid graves: "I lingered around them, under that benign sky; watched the moths fluttering among the heath and hare-bells; listened to the soft wind breathing through the grass; and wondered how anyone could ever imagine unquiet slumbers for the sleepers in that quiet earth." It's been almost 160 years since the guns of the Civil War were silenced and its survivors found their way to Glendora.

Marquita Shepperd Barber in the Glendora Historical Museum, 2009

The Clardy-Engelhardt Legacy

Dr. August Engelhardt, c. 1897

Rosa Clardy Engelhardt, c. 1897

Most of us have casual relationships with employees in local businesses. We greet each other, comment on the weather, and move on. Occasionally we run into them elsewhere — say, in a department store — and they look so unfamiliar in a new setting that we forget their names and can't remember how we know them. But sometimes, we are lucky to have a relationship grow into a friendship. Such was my experience with the late Bob Hillman.

I'd known Bob for years before the day he saw the *Glendoran* magazine on the passenger seat of my car. He owned R.A. Hillman Enterprises in Arcadia, and I took my car to him for servicing. I often asked for his advice on vehicle maintenance, and as time went on, we chatted about mutual friends, discussed the intricacies of auto repair, and laughed away the world's problems.

But that day in 2009 when he explained his Glendora roots, I found myself telling him that his great-grandmother attended my great-grandmother's wedding and gave her a mustard dish. It's a

Wedding picture, Dr. August and Rosa Engelhardt, Missouri, May 1887

Bob Hillman of R.A. Hillman Enterprises, Arcadia, 2009

complex story of pioneer families intermarrying, but in the late 1800s, the De Shields, Caseys, and Shepperds were cousins to the Engelhardts, Kamphefners, and Clardys. Maintaining my vehicle became a more interesting errand when we could talk about our family histories.

Bob's parents were Marjorie and Robert Clinton Hillman of Arcadia; his grandparents Edith and Edward Love of Los Angeles; his great-grandparents, Alberta and William Giles Clardy of Glendora. And William's sister was Rosa Clardy who married Dr. August Engelhardt. He was the postmaster of Glendora in 1888 and the doctor who delivered most of the settlers' babies with Rosa's help. In other words, his great-granduncle delivered all three of my great-grandparents' children.

I can see you marveling over these revelations.

If not, would you be interested to know that dynamite was once sold in the Engelhardt store? The original settlers of the Azusa Valley shared life's joys and explosions with a camaraderie that still flourishes in this town, and their stories overlap.

The Engelhardt children, about ten of them, came to the United States from Germany in 1848 with their mother Anna Mary Deal to join their father Henry who had arrived two years earlier. Henry and his brothers wanted to get out of the German army because the Kaiser kept waging war. The only way to escape was to marry while on furlough. Two of the brothers did. Of course, by immigrating to the United States, they ended up in the Civil War.

The family settled in Indiana where their son John Peter was born on September 29, 1849, attended school, and grew up speaking both English and German. While there is no account of John's participation in the Civil War, his older brother Henry D. was injured serving with the 83rd Indiana Infantry in the Battle of Dallas and was hospitalized for two months. Henry also served in the Vicksburg campaign and other important engagements.

A horticulturist at heart, John left his family at nineteen to grow fruit in Trimble County, Kentucky. He continued his agricultural pursuits in Platte County, Missouri, before settling for three years in Compton, California. Then in 1882, he found his way to the Azusa Valley. Here, he bought fourteen acres of land north of Palm Drive and then homesteaded 160 acres of mountain land that he turned into a horticultural ranch called Englewild. Today, if you drive up Rose to Englewild Drive, you can see lovely foliage and exotic plants, punctuated with gorgeous palms, on the hillside above the housing development. Though his home and barn are gone, you can see John's horticultural handiwork above you. That year, he traveled east to visit his family and to bring his sister Rose back with him. The following year, his brother Henry D. joined them here before Glendora existed.

The original valley settlers didn't know which crops would grow and had no way of getting water except to carry it down from the foothills in barrels. John experimented with citrus and other fruits, grapes

Engelhardt home, c. 1885

Henry D. Engelhardt's family, c. 1885

and apricots, on his ranch and later developed a system of pruning lemon trees that won him a following of orchardists.

His experience with water is well-documented but worth repeating. In the early 1880s, he and John Bender tried to move water from their canyon springs to lowland reservoirs through bamboo pipelines. They used a long iron poker to burn out the centers of the bamboo trunks, sealed the joints between the pipes together with pitch or pine tar, and laid them from the foothills to the valley. This method was successful until the joints leaked and bamboo sprouted in the foothills.

Then William Bryant Cullen started working with a man who knew a way to make a seamless and jointless cement pipe. This pipeline was the first successful means of transporting water from Englewild Canyon to a reservoir that was located where Cullen Avenue and Sierra Madre Boulevard intersect now. After that, John Engelhardt was able to construct his own small metal pipeline that delivered about sixty gallons a day to his own land. Other settlers followed their lead, so there were many pipelines coming down from the foothills before the town became a reality.

By the time George D. Whitcomb showed up to found the town of Glendora, John was almost forty and ready for a business challenge, so he bought land in preparation for his younger brother August's arrival.

His brother was to become a major asset to Glendora. He served as its doctor, postmaster, grocer, druggist, school board member, mayor, landowner, and citrus grower when the town needed his skills. August

Engelhardt was born in Ohio County, Indiana, on August 28, 1856 and was raised as a farmer. From there, he moved to Kentucky with his parents for five years, then in 1873 to Platte County, Missouri. At twenty, he started to nurture more academic interests and enrolled in Lane University in Lecompton, Kansas, graduating in 1878. He completed instruction at the Commercial College at Leavenworth, then returned to his home in Missouri where he taught in public schools. When the field of medicine caught his attention, a medical practitioner in that state took him on as an apprentice. In 1884, he received a diploma from the Physio-Medical Institute in Cincinnati, Ohio, and returned to Missouri to practice. He wasn't there long.

Dr. August Engelhardt and Rosa Clardy married on May 19, 1887, in Missouri and arrived in Glendora on the new Santa Fe railroad on May 26, 1887. About eleven years older than his wife, August was ready to establish himself in the medical profession, so his arrival was timely. The new town would need a doctor. It would also need a more formal post office.

On the day that the Land Company sold lots in the new town, his brother John bought one on the northeast corner of Vista Bonita and Whitcomb Avenues that would become the site of the new post office. Believing that John had chosen land on what would be the main street, he and August built the first store there. The grocery section was on one side, the drug store on the other, and the living quarters were behind the building. The brothers carried a stock of crockery, flour, feed, paints, oils, fancy goods, and jewelry, in addition to medicines. They also sold dynamite to miners who were still panning for gold and other metals in the foothills. Soon, they were running the post office.

In July 1887, William Bryant Cullen realized the importance of doing business in a central location, so he made August Engelhardt a deputy postmaster, and the post office was moved from the Cullen home to the Engelhardt brothers' store, making it the first post office to be named Glendora.

The first post office was called Alosta and its brief history started with a man named Fuller. In 1883, Harrison Fuller had petitioned Washington for a post office that he named Alosta after his daughter Anna Losta, an opera singer. Between 1883 and 1887, W.B. Cullen volunteered to serve as the postmaster and sorted the mail on his back porch in a J. & P. Coats chest designed to hold spools of thread. The thread box was an informal arrangement, as was the Alosta name, but because the naming of a post office is the naming of an area, old town Glendora was once called Alosta. After he'd purchased the land for his town, Whitcomb saw to it that the old post office was closed, and the new post office — still the thread box — was named after his wife Leadora and the glen behind his home. As a result, Major George E. Gard, a land speculator, was free to use the name Alosta for both the town he established one mile south of Glendora and its post office. Today, letters postmarked Alosta are collectors' items.

In 1888, August Engelhardt received the appointment of postmaster. The Glendora *Signal* ran this article on March 22.

> Dr. A. E. Engelhardt is now postmaster, indeed, having just received a bran [*sic*] new commission from Washington. We had thought to send him to regulate the strike, as far as it affected the mails at least, but were afraid that even his newly conferred dignity wouldn't be sufficient. He has proven himself a faithful officer and is giving general satisfaction in the discharge of his official duties. Glendora will be made a money order office in June, a convenience we will anxiously await. The lock boxes ordered for our post office are very slow in coming. The first order made last fall was lost on the way, after a long delay in shipment. . .

The world was much slower when the town doctor had time to be the postmaster, too. Like W.B. Cullen, August Engelhardt would have known all his neighbors because they walked onto his property to pick up their mail, addressed with only the recipient's name and the name of the post office. There were no streets and no house numbers.

The ability to mail a money order from a post office was important then. Before Glendora was established, the valley's residents would walk or ride on horseback or in carriages to the Azusa Post Office to mail money to their families on the East Coast. While Cullen was acting postmaster of the Alosta branch, he himself mailed money in Azusa and signed the registry as a resident of Azusa — because all valley residents were Azusans before 1887. But he did not sign that he was a resident of Alosta, perhaps believing the name identified only the postal service, the thread box on his back porch.

Within a year, the Engelhardt brothers needed more space for the store and post office, so they added a second story for living quarters. When Rosa was pregnant, though, she didn't want to climb upstairs, so she and August moved from their quarters above the store into one of the twin houses, built in 1885 by the Davis brothers and now located at 211 and 215 E. Virginia Ave. Thomas Kamphefner, who had married the Engelhardts' sister Rose, had built his own store just north of theirs to sell general hardware and some groceries.

It's almost impossible to portray the richness of the past in any history book, but consider this paragraph about business competition from Ruth Pratt Kimball's history of Glendora:

August and Rosa Engelhardt with their sons,
Ernest, Walter, and Clayton, c. 1907

> Substantial and dependable were these mercantile centers of the new town, but for real excitement and pleasure, especially to the younger members of the households, were the intermittent visits of the stores on wheels–miniature box cars, horse drawn, with sides that opened to display the treasures within–treasures of yardage, notions and kitchenware that were craftily traded for eggs and ranch produce. Of equal importance were the visits of the Chinese vegetable and fish merchants, the latter with two baskets slung from a pole carried across his shoulders.

Ironically, the most stable of the early businesses proved to be transient. Both the Engelhardt and Kamphefner stores were moved to Michigan Avenue (now Glendora) when it became the main street. Both burned. The Engelhardt building was destroyed in 1896, in the first of a series of four fires. It must have seemed a normal business practice to sell dynamite to miners, but when it exploded, it cracked the glass in the windows of homes and businesses throughout the town.

In the museum, a note from John B. Craig, M.D. states that his father, Dr. W.H. Craig, lived in Glendora and practiced medicine with August Engelhardt in 1895 and 1896. He writes, "In the latter year, their offices and drug store burned down, the fire resulting from a spreading fire from the adjoining Justice of the Peace office. This fire so discouraged my father, it having practically cleaned him out financially, that he moved to North Ontario, now named Upland, where he started out anew." For a while afterwards, Dr. Engelhardt practiced medicine from his home.

The Kamphefner store and Odell building burned along with the post office not long after the Engelhardt fire, and the next year saw two other fires. One burned the town hall and Miller's feed store; another burned Bidwell's building where John Daley had a law office.

August Engelhardt became more interested in the citrus industry as he got older, and he had extensive real estate dealings throughout southern California. He would plant lemon and orange orchards, then sell them to investors once they were established. By 1915, his home was a five-acre tract surrounded by orange and lemon trees. He also owned a ten-acre lemon grove in this valley, twenty acres supervised by his son Clayton at Corona, and a forty-acre fruit ranch at Exeter in Tulare County that his son Ernest managed. His son Walter earned a law degree in 1914 from the University of California and opened offices in Los Angeles.

As the mayor from 1912-1916, August was responsible for the commercial and educational development of the community. He supervised the installation of ornamental street lights and eight miles of electric light. The old water system was purchased and bond money was approved for its expansion and modernization during his terms of office. With W.G. Hall, he formed the Glendora Independent Water Company and sank seven wells, among other achievements.

Dr. August Engelhardt and Rosa raised Clayton (1889), Ernest (1890), and Walter (1892) in the family home at 120 W. Colorado St. August prospered as a citrus rancher and land developer until his death at sixty-eight on November 18, 1924. His son Ernest and his family stayed on the Colorado ranch when Rosa moved to a smaller home on Vermont. All were active in the Christian Church. Today one of the Engelhardts' great-granddaughters Catherine Black lives on Route 66.

There are plenty of Engelhardts on the 1900 United States Federal Census. By that time, John Peter had married Rose Hess from Columbus, Ohio, who dropped the "d" from the Englehart name and, at forty, gave birth to their son Orton who later invented the Rain Bird sprinkler. The Englehart homestead was torn down and developed in 1990, but the Glendora Preservation Foundation dismantled, then rebuilt Orton's shed in Centennial Heritage Park to commemorate his achievements.

Henry D. married Katherine "Kate" Kamphefner in 1870 in Missouri, and they raised six children, including Jesse whom they adopted, at their home near what is now the northeast corner of Minnesota and Virginia. The children were Anna Mary Stower (1870), John Gracen (1873), Clara B. Rietzke (1875), Nellie May Cullen (1877), August "Gusty" E. (1886), and Jesse T. (1893). Both John Gracen and Gusty died as children. The family home still exists and still belongs to the family. Four generations of family members have lived in it. Kate and Henry's great-granddaughter Karen Cullen and her husband Dan Wilshire live there now.

But the other side of the Dr. Engelhardt story belongs to his wife Rosa Clardy. In addition to raising a family of three boys and helping in the Engelhardt brothers' store, as she couldn't have failed to do, Rosa also helped her husband deliver Glendorans' babies.

She and her brother William Giles Clardy were born in Kansas in the late 1860s to Lucrecia Ann Todd and James Clardy. In a second union, their mother married Thomas McCormick and moved, first to Missouri, then west to Covina with him and another daughter after both Rosa and William G. were settled in Glendora.

Bill Clardy was a teenager when he arrived in Glendora to visit his sister Rosa and her husband August on their citrus ranch. It's no surprise that he stayed. He earned money doing odd jobs around town, and one of them was to drive Whitcomb's water wagon.

It wasn't a bad job. Ruth Pratt Kimball says in her history of the town that George Dexter Whitcomb came here to fish in 1885 and found food and refreshment at Harrison Fuller's home. Charmed with the location and envisioning a town, he asked to see Fuller's water supply. He must have found it adequate because he later bought about two hundred acres from W.B. Cullen, James J. West, and Henry D. Engelhardt at forty dollars an acre. He wanted to start a town.

The Glendora Water Company would eventually lay pipes under the streets and distribute an estimated fifty-six thousand feet of pipeline to homebuilders. Until that happened, Whitcomb wanted to settle the disputes about water, so he sent a man in a horse-drawn wagon into the foothills every day to bring water down and distribute it. Glendorans would put containers of all shapes and sizes outside for this precious delivery and would receive an amount commensurate with the number of people in their homes. Bill Clardy's customers would have been appreciative.

Glendorans built several dams in the foothills to collect water that was piped down to the valley both for irrigation and domestic use. Bill had another job working on one of those dams. At the end of the day, he would walk home from the mountains above the town, according to Bob Hillman, his great-grandson. He also drove supplies in a buckboard across the desert to Mojave.

When he'd earned enough money, Bill Clardy bought his own citrus ranch on Grand Avenue next to Oakdale Cemetery where he and Alberta raised their family. Until recently, the home stood within the Oakdale Cemetery gates, the ranch subdivided long ago.

Many families moved west to Glendora in the mid-1880s, and Alberta Chadwick's family was another one. Mary Gregson and James

Chadwick were living outside of Manchester, England, in about 1885 when they decided to move to the United States with their two daughters, Alberta Louisa, 5, and Alice, 10. Their brother George was already in California performing with the Barnum and Bailey Circus. Settling first in Minnesota, the Chadwick family moved to the Azusa Valley within a year and made it their home.

Their daughter Alberta looks about twelve in a class picture taken outside the Glendora Grammar school in about 1892 with her classmates of varied ages. The male teacher in the photo looks as stern as he can with his arms folded in front of him and his frown aimed at his students. A female teacher in glasses stares straight into the camera, but her hands rest on two young boys' shoulders as though they were the ones she expected to misbehave. Alberta is in the fourth row, the fourth student from the right.

At sixteen, she was introduced to twenty-six-year-old William Clardy, and they married in the original Christian Church where it stood on the northeast corner of Wabash and Bennett in June 1897. After more than twenty years in Glendora, Alberta and William Clardy moved to Los Angeles with their two children, Edith and Edwin James, but the family still considered Glendora their home. In 1910, William got a job in a powerhouse for the electric street cars and worked there until he retired. Later, the Clardys moved to Monrovia where they celebrated their sixtieth wedding anniversary. All four are buried in Oakdale Cemetery, Glendora.

Glendora Grammar School, c. 1892. Alberta Chadwick in dark dress with white bow, fourth row, third from right.

Clardy ranch home, located inside Oakdale Cemetery grounds, c. 1990

William Giles Clardy and Alberta Chadwick, wedding picture, 1897

Clardy, Love, and Hillman families, 1950s. Alberta and William Clardy seated center of second row; Bob and Linda Hillman, bottom right; Mike Love of the Beach Boys, center back row, blond; Edward Milton Love, the father of both Mike and Stan Love may be the tall man in the back row.

As a miscellaneous note, the Clardy's son-in-law Edward Love owned a sheet metal company that supplied kitchen appliances to Sambo's, Denny's, Bob's Big Boy, and other restaurants. One of the Clardys' great-grandsons, Mike Love, became a member of the Beach Boys. He's in the back row, center, of a family picture taken in the 1950s with his cousins and his great-grandparents Alberta and William. Brothers Mike and Stan Love are cousins to Brian, Dennis, and Carl Wilson, the other Beach Boys. Also pictured may be his father Edward Milton Love and his brother Stan Love who had a noteworthy career in professional basketball. Stan's son Kevin Love was also an NBA champion. (I love the miracle of researching trivia.)

Not only was Bertie Chadwick a guest at my great-grandparents' wedding, she was there with her mother Mary. And in a letter from my great-grandmother to her sister Meda dated January 1, 1922, she writes that Alberta's son Edwin Clardy had dropped by their house in L.A. to visit with other friends on Christmas Day. What an amazing collection of minutiae we leave behind us.

Glendora's Water Dowser
William Russell Shepperd and Alice May Kammerdiener

William Russell Shepperd, 1864-1940

Alice May Kammerdiener, 1875-1951

All my Azusa Valley ancestors were concerned about water.

When John Casey and his son-in-law William Jasper De Shields rented land from Henry Dalton in the early 1860s, water rights came with the rentals. Both Casey's son and De Shields served as valley water commissioners during the 1870s while Henry Dalton's lawsuit against the settlers continued, as alive and well as Dalton himself. They were still on the commission after his death on January 1, 1884.

The Shepperd side of my family started arriving in 1886 when Whitcomb was laying out the town of Glendora, setting its boundaries, planning its streets, and finally submitting its map to the county office in September 1887. William Russell Shepperd followed his birth family here in 1891.

Bill Shepperd was a water dowser. In other words, he could find underground water by using a forked stick, a skill he'd learned in Kansas. Few published sources confirm his dowsing. When one early settler was interviewed for Helen Bettin's book, *This I Remember*, she said that a Mr. Shepperd owned a water witch, a device used for finding underground water. Not much of a reference. But a newspaper article that his granddaughter Marquita Shepperd Barber treasured gave Bill credit for finding many of the springs in the valley, and attested to the existence of the forked stick that he used to find them.

Fenwick Warner, a Glendora realtor and also a water dowser, was the subject of an article that appeared in the *San Gabriel Valley Tribune* on Sunday, March 25, 1979. The *Glendoran* magazine published another piece about him in the May/Jun 1991 issue. As a young man, Warner got a job as a chemist for the George W. Fuhr Fertilizer Company in Azusa. During the Depression, his boss told him he'd have to let Warner go unless he went out to Alosta Avenue, now Route 66, and sold some manure to W.R. Shepperd, a citrus grower.

After four hours of his best sales banter, Warner was subjected to another ultimatum. Bill Shepperd said he'd buy manure from him only if he could find an underground stream on his property with a forked stick. Fearing for his job, Warner took the challenge. He was a trained chemist with an interest in geology and knew there was no way he'd find water, but he didn't want to lose his job.

"Sure enough," Warner said, "the stick dipped and Shepperd said that's where the water was so I made the sale and my job was saved."

Warner went on to practice professional dowsing and was able to find water in many remote desert areas. Like most dowsers, he never figured out why dowsing works, but his confidence in it was such that he'd sometimes bet his employer double his fee or nothing. "To me, it's the nearest thing to an all-out miracle that we have," he said.

In the article, Warner pointed out that "many of the important wells that irrigated San Gabriel Valley citrus fields in the early years of the century were found by Shepperd, Lee Bashor of Covina, or other local dowsers." So why didn't historians give them credit for these finds?

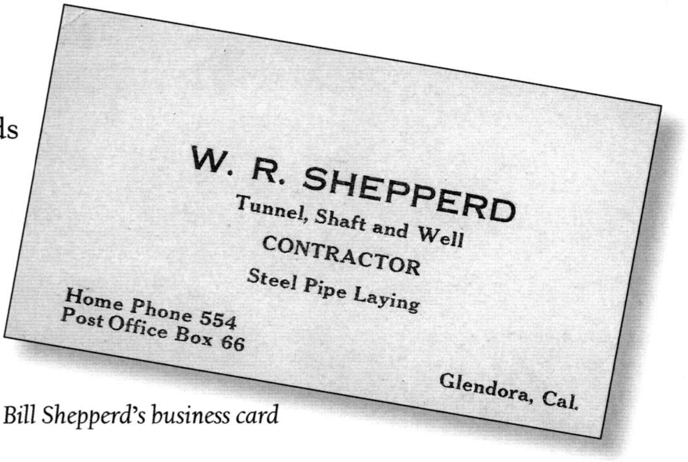

Bill Shepperd's business card

Possibly for the same reason that Rob Thompson, an engineer and third-generation dowser who once owned the largest individual drilling company in California, won't divulge the names of the vintners who hire him to find wells in their Sonoma vineyards. When I interviewed him in 2010, he didn't want to embarrass his clientele. Americans may be reluctant to let the public know they rely on dowsing to find sources of underground water on their properties, but it doesn't bother Rob.

When I called to ask him about dowsing, he said first, "I'm a licensed engineer." And he's a successful dowser. Even today. Thompson wasn't keeping track of his successes, but he compared himself to another local dowser who claimed about eighty-two percent accuracy.

Rob explained his process: he uses metal stainless steel rods to locate water, but he says other dowsers use other things. He puts two rods in the ground in a neutral position, then meditates and relaxes in that zone. He circles, holding the rods out and downward until they cross. The higher they cross, the stronger the source. Then he moves in that direction.

When he finds a source, he knows he's found it. He just knows. Then he pinpoints the center vein by walking at angles and driving in a stake, though there are other techniques. His degree of success is determined by the volume of water he locates. For example, if he isn't on the vein, he may locate a source that yields ten gallons of water at eighty feet. But on the vein, he might locate a yield of twenty-five gallons of water at 110 to 130 feet. At some point, there's no more water. This was Rob's explanation more than ten years ago. Since then, his business has taken off as the drought in California has gotten worse. Today, Rob has expanded his challenges to finding the locations of shipwrecks, oil and gas deposits, minerals, and more.

Thompson is interested in the work that scientists are doing to harness subtle energies and says geologists who find water in more conventional ways are dowsing at a subliminal level. His website is a fine source of information on dowsing. Rob also teaches dowsing and has offered to demonstrate for me the next time I'm in Sonoma. I'm anxious to take him up on his offer since I may have the Shepperd dowsing gene and because I've had no luck on my own in the Los Angeles Arboretum with two coat hangers and no instruction. Training helps.

Glendoran Bill Shepperd learned to dowse near Topeka, Kansas, where he was born on June 12, 1864, about ten months before Lincoln was killed and the Civil War officially ended. The earliest Kansas pioneers, his mother among them, relied on dowsers to locate water on the plains because those lands with water were more valuable. Young Shepperd showed both an interest and a talent for using a water witch. There is no record of his teachers, but since dowsing has been used in Europe for thousands of years, his teacher was probably an immigrant.

Bill Shepperd and his second wife, Alice, c. 1895

When his family followed his sister Meda Ella and her new husband George Bennett Whitcomb to Glendora in 1887, William stayed in Kansas, then moved to Indian Territory that later became Oklahoma. According to his sister Maggie's memoirs, he had married an Indian, "a scandalous thing to do at that time."

His granddaughter Marquita Shepperd Barber knew nothing about his first wife, and his divorce papers dated November 2, 1891, in Oklahoma Territory reveal little except that his wife "on or about September 1, 1890 willfully deserted the plaintiff without any cause whatever, and that said defendant from that date up to the time of the filing of the petition herein has continued to live separate from the plaintiff and refused at all times during said time to live with the plaintiff as his wife."

His divorce coincided with the removal of Indians to reservations. If she was, in fact, an Indian, her lifestyle changed dramatically after Oklahoma Territory was organized in 1890. Indian tribes did not fare well after the Civil War because their tribal governments had signed treaties with the Confederacy. Their penalty for siding with the South was the loss of half their lands. It was a punishment that was never exacted against the Confederacy itself, but it meant that vast numbers of Indians were displaced. If nothing else, the papers prove the marriage was short and its dissolution may have prompted his move to California in 1891. Bill would have rejoined his family in Glendora.

No one knows how he met Alice May Kammerdiener, but she was to be his lifelong spouse.

Alice was born in Scammon, Kansas, on January 4, 1875. She told her granddaughter Marquita two stories about her youth. As a young woman Alice had gone with her parents to Indian Territory, later Oklahoma, where they visited a reservation. An Indian offered to give her father

William Russell Shepperd and Alice May Kammerdiener, 1896

twenty ponies for her hand, but her father turned him down. As a farewell gift, the Indian beaded some moccasins for Alice that have been passed down to one of her great-granddaughters, Mary Frantz.

While she was still young, Alice May married an older man named Hinkle, and they went to live in a dugout in either Kansas or Indian Territory. Dugouts were cramped and primitive dwellings on arid plains where there were no trees to use for log cabins. Instead, the early settlers dug into the sides of hills or ravines, leaving small openings for windows or doors. Sometimes prairie turf was used to make sod bricks to add a front wall and roof. Alice started her married life in one of these structures.

One night, she thought she heard someone outside the dugout, and when she went outside to check, she saw a white presence. When she fled back inside to her husband, she found he had died.

This incident may well have prompted Alice to travel west with her parents and siblings when they joined a wagon train. She was married again in California to a man named Joseph Jackson Killian. It was another brief marriage. Still only about twenty, Alice had a son named Roscoe who died of pneumonia when he was about six months old. She and her husband divorced in Los Angeles, and six days later, on June 12, 1896, she married William Russell Shepperd in San Bernardino County. This marriage — her third, his second — lasted. They may have met while she was a waitress at the Riverside Mission Inn and when she was still young enough to think a customer was cussing when he asked for "E-dam cheese."

Bathing picture (l-r): Unidentified man, William Shepperd standing, and Frank Shepperd, c. 1885

Though the 1900 census finds the young couple living in Glendora with her mother Lucinda Allen and brother Fred, they spent their early married years in Arcata in Humboldt County where two of their four children were born. The four children were Juanita, Waldo, Frieda, and Arlone.

When the Shepperds returned to Glendora in 1909, they were coming back to a town filled with relatives. Bill purchased a citrus grove on Alosta Avenue, and like many early Glendorans, the family lived in a makeshift barn on the property until the house could be built near the dirt road that Alosta was then. The house still stands at 726 Route 66.

Adults on the porch (l-r): Meda Shepperd Whitcomb, Jennie Shepperd, Olive Shepperd Kamphefner, Alice Kammerdiener Shepperd, Henry Kammerdiener with crutch, and William Russell Shepperd. Juanita Shepperd is the child on the left, c. 1910.

Juanita Shepperd standing with girls basketball team, Glendora, 1922

Bill Shepperd started work with Los Angeles County Flood Control and was known in Glendora as a contractor and water developer. His card says he was a tunnel, shaft, and well contractor. He could also lay steel pipes. Of course, he had his citrus groves, too, both orange and lemon trees. The Shepperd property had Dalton Wash as its south border with the South Hills across from it. His daughter Juanita, her friend Liz Sturtevant, and a boy named Otto Georgi whose father owned the midsection of the face of South Hills, tramped all over those hills as children.

As far as water-dowsing is concerned, I want to believe it works in the same way that I have learned to depend on my computer. How does it work? The most

W. R. Shepperd Services Held

Funeral services for William R Shepperd, 75, resident of Glendora for more than 30 years, were conducted Thursday afternoon at the Glendora Christian Church. Rev. George W. Crain officiated and interment followed at Oakdale Cemetery with arrangements in charge of White's Funeral Home.

Mr. Shepperd died at his home at 740 East Alosta Avenue Tuesday morning after an illness which had kept him in failing health for the past 18 months. He was widely known in this city as a contractor and water developer and was affiliated with the Los Angeles County Flood Control District for more than ten years. Since his retirement he has been an active rancher and citrus grower.

Born in Topeka, Kansas, on June 12, 1864, Mr. Shepperd came to California in 1891, establishing his residence in Glendora in 1909.

The deceased is survived by his wife, Mrs. Alice Shepperd; three daughters, Mrs. Juanita Stiles of North Hollywood, Mrs. Freda Rich of San Dimas and Mrs. Arlone Rhinehart of La Verne; one son, W. R. Shepperd Jr., of Glendora; three sisters, Mrs. M. DeShields of Glendale, Mrs. Cora Campbell of Compton and Mrs. Olive Kamphefner of Glendora; and one brother, Frank Shepperd of Los Angeles

Bill Shepperd's obituary, 1940

knowledgeable of technicians start their answers with two machines talking to each other but ignore the miracle of such a feat. Nor have I heard an explanation of acupuncture, though I've had treatments that eliminated both pain and stress. Bill Shepperd was a water dowser, and I like the idea that there was such a man in my family. Men who have ways with underground springs are gifted and few.

The descendants of Bill and Alice Shepperd and those of Bill's sister Maggie and John Walter De Shields. I'm wearing a skirt in the front row, and my younger and shorter brother, Richard Gregory Staral, is wearing dark pants and standing to my right. My mother Rae Staral is behind me with dark hair and a beaded poodle on her shoulder. 1957.

The Memoirs of Frances De Shields Metzger

A Childhood in Glendora, 1896–1910

Part One

Frances De Shields, c. 1909

My grandmother, Frances De Shields, knew how to whistle. Really whistle. One of the highlights of my third grade year at Eagle Rock Elementary School was the day she showed off for my teacher Mr. Harris. My class was walking into the empty hallway after lunch, and he stopped to talk with Frankie, as my brother and I called her. She laughed at something he said, and he must have challenged her. Here? I can still see the doubt in her expression. Then she stuck her index finger and thumb in her mouth and let 'er rip.

The sound of her whistle was wonderful. It became a presence in the hallway, first a strong tone expanding, then a blast. It bounced around the cavernous school hallway and seemed to hang there while curious children and other teachers appeared in doorways. Mr. Harris laughed, delighted, and I could see that everyone loved Frankie's tomboy talent. I've never heard anyone whistle the way she could, and when she was asked, she bragged that she'd developed her gift in Glendora orchards.

There were plenty of children to play with in the early 1900s when Frances De Shields was a child. She had two younger brothers, Bob and Glen, and plenty of cousins including the Kamphefner and Shepperd children and many school friends like Lora West, Ruth Gnagy, Chester Olnstead, and Bruce Clark.

In 1977 when Frankie was eighty-one years old, I asked her to write her memoirs. She did. The first notebook tells the story of her Glendora childhood and brings the town to life. Her candor may surprise you, but she was a pianist for silent films during the Roaring Twenties. By the 1930s she had her own radio shows on a few Los Angeles stations. Even at ninety-five, she was still feisty and stylish with platinum blonde hair, and she'd outlived two husbands. I'm compelled to edit her spelling and grammar a bit, but I want to share her words with you. My notes are in brackets.

I was born in Glendora in 1896. Babies were being born at home at that time, and the town doctor attended. I was born in my uncle Frank's home, a boxy two-story house. [217 E. Leadora Ave.] My mother had an upstairs front bedroom. Dr. Engelhardt was the popular doctor. His wife was later my Sunday school teacher and attended the pioneer picnics many years later. That's another story.

My parents were Mary Margaret Shepperd and John Walter De Shields. They were called Maggie and Walt. We lived in a small house across from the Christian Church to which our family belonged. Maybe my brothers were born there. I'm not sure. I remember my mother rocking me, waiting for the doctor to come and lance "a gathering," we called it, on my neck under my chin. I must have been two or three years old. I can still see that room, Mom putting me on the bed in pain while the doctor lanced whatever it was. I still have a slightly visible scar.

We must have lived there quite a while as I remember going to Sunday school and Mom singing in the choir. Everyone went to church and Sunday school as there was nothing else to do and it was fun. Some of my cousins and friends went to the Methodist church. I only remember the two churches. [The Christian Church was on the northeast corner of Wabash and Bennett at that time.]

The next place we lived I remember clearly. It was on Vermont, south of the wash. Uncle Henry and Aunt Ollie lived north of the wash

John Walter and Maggie De Shields on their wedding day, July 3, 1895

towards the mountains. The wash was a huge, deep riverbed through the center of town, like a big ditch. In the winter it would fill up from the rains and overflow, and everyone used to go see the rushing, dangerous waters. It was rough getting across it, and I believe there was a bridge on the main street. [The Kamphefner home was located at the entrance of Dalton Canyon.]

Glendora was a beautiful country town with orange, lemon, tangerine, and grapefruit trees. The town was made up of orange groves everywhere. There was a packing house across the railroad tracks near the station. Mom and my Aunt Matt [Mattye De Shields] packed oranges day after day when we lived in that house on Vermont.

The Whitcombs were the first people of Glendora. They made the laws of the town. There were still no bars or saloons within the limits of Glendora. Of course, one doesn't have to go far to find them now.

The streets of Glendora were lined with pepper trees dripping with red berries that we loved to rake up and burn. Streets were not paved or black-topped. There were no street lights, and if families visited at night or there was a celebration, the man of the house carried a coal oil lantern. No one had electric lights in the home. Lamps burned coal oil and had a wick that had to be trimmed and lighted with a match, and a glass chimney was placed over the flame. The lamps were filled and chimneys cleaned every day. They finally got electricity in the homes. We had beautiful lamps as well, like the Tiffany lamps — painted or stained glass.

Ethel Arenshield and Frances with her father on his raft in Big Dalton Dam. Frances didn't know how to swim.

Glendora was at the foot of the mountains. The southern part was overlooked by the Alosta hills. A little place was there called Alosta. My Uncle Willie, the youngest of Mom's brothers lived at the foot of the Alosta Hills in an orange grove. He owned many acres there, leased out to the orange pickers' association. We were not allowed to pick them from the ground as they went for orange juice. They had four children: Juanita, Waldo, Frieda, and Arlone. Aunt Allie was Willie's wife, a nice lady. [William Shepperd's home, 726 E. Route 66.]

When we kids were five, six, and seven, we used to wander all over these beautiful Alosta hills picking wildflowers and ferns. The flowers were Johnny-jump-ups, buttercups, paintbrushes, beautiful yellow California poppies. I wonder if they still grow there.

Mom, Dad, and we three kids used to climb the mountains to the north of Glendora. There were narrow trails to follow. We always loved this as Mom always had a big picnic bag packed. We would go to the Big Dalton Canyon where there was a lake and running water, lots of it. Dad built a raft and took us kids and our friends for rides.

On the Fourth of July, our family and friends would gather at Uncle Frank's house where I was born and have a whopper of a picnic in the backyard. There were tall trees there, plenty of room. We kids took

Bob, Glen, and Frances. Their mother finally had to cut Glen's curls into a boy's style.

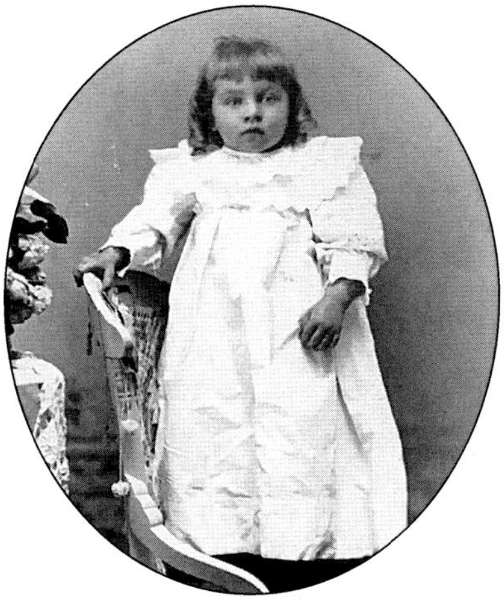

Maudie Shepperd died of peritonitis in about 1902.

turns turning the ice cream freezers. Ice cream does not taste like that now — pure cream and fresh fruit.

Aunt Alice, Uncle Frank's first wife, made the best tamales I have ever tasted, full of meat and goodies, not the mushy stuff you get now. She made them to sell very often by request. [Alice Chadwick.]

Winifred, Jennie, and Marvel were their kids, my cousins. Maudie, their first born, died when I was about three or four years old. It left me with a trauma about death. She was just a little girl, and they had her laid out in their living room. I was playing under the trees at the side of our house on Vermont in the mud, making houses and tracks, and Mom called me in and told me Maudie had died. It seemed like the end of the world to me then.

I played there a lot. I would fill a big crockery pitcher with water from a faucet that was right there and empty it to make the mud things. One time I dropped that heavy pitcher, filled, on my toes. Such pain for many days, I had to go to the doctor. The big toe was crushed.

We had a big backyard there. Dad always had a yard of vegetables. He was a partner in the grocery business with Mr. Hall. Dad bought his own store and bought this house. [The Glendora Market was downstairs from Glenn Odell's dental office.]

Aunt Matt, Dad's younger sister, lived with us. We must have lived there a long time as I remember I learned to ride Aunt Matt's bicycle there, and I used to steal her dime novels from under her mattress and read them. Mom did not approve of dime novels. I was too young but very curious. I know now they were just love stories, and Aunt Matt was in her twenties and not married yet. Mom bought my big old upright piano when I was about seven years old. She started me out on basic music and a teacher from Pomona gave me classical lessons.

There were quite a few houses on Vermont, both north and south of the wash. Mr. Martin, an old man, and his two daughters lived on one side of us. Kenneth [Kamphefner] was a great one to make up words about people. Kenneth made up this poem about Mr. Martin. "Mrs. Nichols made some pickles on a rainy day. Mr. Martin came in fartin' and blew them all away." We kids would get the biggest kick out of that. I still laugh at it. Mr. Martin was a funny old man.

Our neighbors across the street had a big wedding. I don't remember the names. When anyone married in Glendora or elsewhere at that time, no one took a trip. They stayed home, so friends or the whole town got together and had a big shivaree — sort of a reception I guess. So that night was a big one. People banged pans, blew whistles, and shot guns. Oh, yeah! My mother and Dad went. They never left us kids at home, and Mom was so frightened she took us three — about two, three, and four — into their clothes closet and sat in the dark until it quieted down and she could take us home. The guns were frightening. So noisy.

Glen was a beautiful child with long curls. Everyone thought he was a girl.

While we lived there, there was a terrible train wreck. I remember it clearly. I was on Aunt Matt's bike. I knew a passenger train was at the station and I could hear another one coming. It was coming fast from the direction of Pomona and crashed into the observation car and right through that car. In fact, it derailed the forward train. People were killed and wounded. It looked awful to see that big engine clobbered into the back of another passenger train. Lots of excitement far into the night. Lanterns bobbing around, etc. Glendora was in the news. Glendora and Azusa are very near to each other, so Azusa people came to the wreck.

There was a small country railroad station like you see in western movies, and old-timers or anyone who had the time enjoyed going to the station to see the trains go by or stop at the tank for water. One or two passenger trains in the daytime and the freights at night. I loved to be in bed and hear the train whistle at night.

Our little white dog Curly was hit by a train. We never knew just how. He got home somehow. He crawled under the house, and so help me he healed himself. He was a dear little dog and we all loved him.

All toilets were at the back of the lot. No house had a toilet inside, so of course, we always had white pots under the beds. They were called *thunder mugs* and had to be emptied every morning and washed out. We kids had to take turns emptying pots. There was nothing to be afraid of, so we would go outside if it wasn't too late. The coyotes were sort of scary. They barked at night from the mountains and hills and often came down to steal chickens and rabbits. It sure made the residents mad.

All backhouse toilets were called *privies*. In the winter, it was a problem. We'd just hopefully find an umbrella and run fast in the mud

Jacob and Jennie Shepperd, Olive Shepperd Kamphefner, and one of her sons in front of the Kamphefner home

and rain. Of course, one could always sit and read a Montgomery Ward catalogue or an old newspaper or look at pictures.

There were no automobiles. If you didn't have a bicycle or horse, you walked. Even at night with a lantern, no street lights — dark as you know what.

I forgot to mention the many times Uncle Frank [Shepperd] piled us in his big wagon with the two horses hitched up to it, and we would go for a picnic in a canyon out of Azusa. We would cross many rocky streams — always many streams in the mountains. Glendora and Azusa were beautiful towns.

Dad's mother and father, William Jasper and Katherine Frances Casey De Shields lived in Glendora — between Azusa and Glendora in a huge orange orchard. Their house was a two-story frame house. I can't remember much about it except we would visit them. [The De Shields are first on the list of title deed owners of the Gladstone House near the corner of Citrus and Gladstone.]

Grandad had planted the first orange grove in the Azusa Valley [in 1874]. The old cemetery where many of my ancestors are buried was not far from their place — sort of on a hill between Azusa and Glendora. [Fairmount Cemetery.] The newer one is on a road between Glendora and Azusa going towards Covina. [Oakdale Cemetery.]

Olive and Henry Kamphefner, c. 1895

Olive and Henry Kamphefner, c. 1905

Mom used to drive us in a horse and buggy to the Covina dentist. There was no dentist in Glendora [until 1908 when Glenn Odell started his dental practice]. I don't remember Grandma and Grandpa [De Shields] moving to Norwalk, but I think it was after the big town fight over water rights. I was too young to know about it.

Most of my memories are of the third place we lived. Mom and Dad sold the place on Vermont and moved north of the wash, closer to Uncle Henry and Aunt Ollie's. [Henry and Olive Kamphefner.] I don't remember if the street had a name. There were big pepper trees across the street, and we kids had a bar and swing. I did all kinds of gymnastics on that bar. Hung by my knees, turnovers, really good at it. I was a tomboy as I had Bob and Glen and their friends and also Kenneth, Ethel's brother. Kenneth and I were great pals. We would go in the fields and hunt squirrels, shoot birds with a sling shot, take them to our backyard, build a fire, put them on a stick, and roast them. We also buried potatoes in the ashes. Some fun. We also would look for holes with a trapdoor over them. Those were tarantula spider holes. I didn't care for that, but Kenneth was an avid trapper. Gads!! What we kids did.

Ethel was three years older than I and the studious type. The Kamphefner house had an attic. It was a two-story frame house. Ethel and I had a town built of cardboard and small boxes all over the attic floor. Our people were paper dolls. It was something to see. We played up there making rooms, cut out furniture, etc. for many hours and days.

The boys used to peek at us, and we'd peek at them. Oh, yeah. They sure would get mad at us.

Uncle Henry had a big yard. The chicken yard was fenced in. There was a path from the back door to the outhouse which had three holes. On one side of the path, there were four big orange trees. To the left of the outhouse was a small barn as they had a cow. They also had a big vegetable garden from the barn to the house. Grandad took care of the garden.

Grandma and Grandpa Shepperd lived with Uncle Henry and Aunt Ollie. They had a big kitchen and dining room with a large old wood stove for cooking. We all had wood stoves — also in the sitting room for heating. There was always wood to chop. They had a nice parlor with an organ, pedaled with the feet, and the room always closed. We were only allowed in there on special occasions, Christmas especially. Uncle Henry always had a big tree and trimmed it in the parlor the night before Christmas, and we kids were kept out of there until Christmas morning when the folding doors were opened. We would come down the stairs in our nightgowns all excited. This was between the years of four to eight, from 1900 to 1904 or 1905.

Aunt Ollie baked bread quite often. One could not go to the store to buy a loaf of bread. I think there were bakeries, but there was no bread in stores. She had a table in the dining room especially for the hot bread. To go there from school on baking day and have Aunt Ollie take off the cloth and tear us off a piece of hot bread and lots of butter is a thing to remember. The dining room had a long table like a banquet table with lots of chairs, not benches. There was Grandma, Grandpa, Aunt Ollie, Uncle Henry, Ethel, Kenneth, and Vernon. Vernon was born later. I don't remember him well. Then, of course, when we kids were there, they had a house full.

I stayed all night with Ethel quite often. We always giggled and laughed far into the night. The folks would yell to us to be quiet. She had her own bedroom upstairs, as did her parents and Kenneth. Grandma and Grandpa Shepperd had a room downstairs. Aunt Ollie had a housekeeper, black, two or three times a week. She washed, cleaned, and cooked. Kenneth called her Bologony.

I loved Ethel's bedroom. We could hear the train whistle at the crossings, the wheels rumbling along and the coyotes barking in the mountains.

We were always back and forth to Aunt Ollie's house even when we lived on Vermont. We had a big red fire engine pulled by the men of the town. If there was a fire, all the church bells and school bells were rung, and everyone would get going. I always wanted to crawl under the bed.

There were orange groves across the street at Uncle Henry's. In fact, the street was orange groves on both sides and a house in the grove with a nice front yard. There was a huge pepper tree in front of the house, and Uncle Henry had chosen the highest limb to put the ropes for a swing. Believe me, that was the highest swing I have ever seen. We could swing as high as the house. It was great.

Grandma had beautiful flowers in the yard. Uncle Henry didn't much like anything she did. He was a gruff man with a walrus mustache. He had a mustache cup and always slurped. We kids giggled with fear.

Layne, this is driving me mad. I see it so clearly in my mind, and it just doesn't read like I see it. It was such a wonderful childhood.

I must not forget this: between 1900 and 1908 — I will try to look this up. A special train was scheduled to go through Glendora and stop at the station with the current President of the United States. What a day that was. I must look that up. The whole town was there, and the President said a few words from the observation car. [When President Taft visited California in 1909, a chair was built for him in Riverside to accommodate his size, so it was probably Taft who spoke from the train.]

Mom's parents, Jennie Porter and Jacob Shepperd had six living children: Maggie (Mom), Aunt [Meda] Ella, Aunt Cora, Aunt Ollie, Uncle Frank, and Uncle Willie. [Two girls died in infancy in Kansas where the family lived during the Civil War.]

The Shepperd sisters, clockwise from left: Olive Kamphefner, Cora Campbell (standing), Maggie De Shields, and Meda Ella Whitcomb, c. 1910

Now the third house I remember.

Dad had bought his grocery store. Grandma Shepperd was with us a lot at this place. Mom was always at the store. We had a large storeroom for groceries at the back so Mom and Dad walled up the front section and made a kitchen and dining room. Many days we kids would rush home from school and have lunch there at noon. Dad and Butch made big batches of Mulligan stew quite often. Butch had the meat, all kinds of meat, and Dad had the vegetables. Any time of day, I could have a big bowl of stew that was sooo good. [Butch may have been an employee.]

One time I was in too big of a rush to the outhouse and fell down the hole, head down, and hung by my knees. I managed to get my hands to the seat and pull myself up, but I was a mess. Someone had left the lid with three toilet holes up against the wall, and me, not thinking I might fall, sat on the edge and over I went. Lunch was not a success. Mom cleaned me up, and I went back to school.

We had five horses. Mom had her own pretty horse named Jake. I used to curry comb mom's horse and help her groom him. Then I could have a ride — always fun. Mom would

Pictures of School Chums

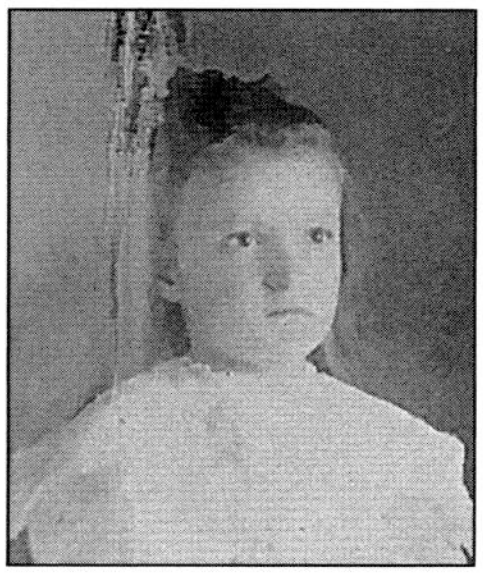

Ruth Gnagy

Bruce Clark, age 10, Jan. 1906

Glen De Shields, Frances' brother

Winifred Shepperd, age 9, Jan. 1906

Ethel Kamphefner, age 11

Chester Olnstead

ride her horse to collect bills. Mom made herself some culottes. She made the pattern herself as there were no patterns to buy. She most probably had the first culottes ever designed. Dad had a long hitching iron in front of the store to tie up horses and buggies when people came to buy groceries. We kids used to have fun doing all kinds of gymnastics on that iron rod. There was a pole on each end to which it was attached four or five feet off the ground. I did flip-flops, hung by the knees, all sorts of things. Girls always wore cotton stockings and, in the winter, long undies wrapped around the legs before the stockings went on and always dresses. No such thing as pants on a girl or woman.

Dad used to let me go with one of our delivery boys to pick up feed and grain and sacks of stuff to sell at Puente. The freight trains stopped there with feed for the farmers. Chickens, horses, cows, rabbits, etc. I had a feeling (at 7 or 8 years old) for this delivery boy, Bob Goodson. He was so good-looking — an older teenager no doubt, and I wanted him to put his hand on my legs which he never did. But I was ashamed because I wore long underwear. I know all about kids' emotions. They talk about it too much now. It was always this way, and I lived in a little country town. Oh, yeah!

Lora West

Louise Hopp, 1908

One girl I used to chum with a lot lived in a big two-story house. She had two older brothers. Her name was Lora West. Her brothers built a tree house in a big tree next to the house. Mr. West had a large ranch — oranges, berries, black and strawberries. Lora and I picked berries for him in season. I would get up at five o'clock and walk in the dark to their place. They always had a nice breakfast, hot muffins, eggs, bacon or homemade sausage. Then out to the fields to pick baskets of blackberries — prickly vines at ten cents a basket. I remember he still owes me twenty cents. Things we remember.

Lora and I were very popular at school as we were taller than most. We played games where sides were chosen like basketball, baseball. Crack the whip was a dandy. A long line of kids holding hands would run fast on the large schoolyard, then stop, and everyone would swing the last one on the line. Believe me, you were lucky if you didn't fall on your face. But it was fun to be the one on the end. Our legs were long, and we could run fast as they swung us. Don't think kids now days know about that game.

Frances, Walter, and Maggie De Shields at a pioneer picnic in the 1940s

The Memoirs of Frances De Shields Metzger

A Childhood in Glendora, 1896–1910

Part Two

A publicity picture of Frances De Shields Patten, c. 1931

I came home from school one day to find my grandmother taking the pictures out of her childhood photo album. I was too late to save the album itself, but I'm still counting my blessings that my grandmother had labeled the backs of all the pictures. When the photos are put together with her 1977 Glendora memoir, the result is both a detailed look at early Glendora and a testament to the quirkiness of human behavior.

Frances De Shields in her mother's hat, c. 1909

You won't be surprised when my grandmother, Frances De Shields Metzger, reveals that people found ways around George D. Whitcomb's no-drinking edict, even despite the activities of the Women's Christian Temperance Union. Nor will it surprise you that some couples bumped along unpaved marital roads occasionally, even in the early 1900s, and survived. Frances' parents were fine examples of individuals who worked out their differences. Here and now, I am still protecting the identity of their innocuous other woman whom I've dubbed Jane Doe of the infamous Doe family.

Every time I read my grandmother's recollections, I find a new mystery. I don't know who Aunt Cary was, perhaps an Inman, and I am still mapping out the locations of the three homes and two stores that were owned and/or run by Walter and Maggie De Shields. Nor can I explain why my grandmother refers to the river between Azusa and Duarte as the Santa Ana River instead of the San Gabriel River. Perhaps a mistake. Yet most of my grandmother's memories fall into place easily.

The rest of her memoirs trace her life in Santa Monica and then L.A. where her piano playing kept her on the periphery of the movie industry. Frankie loved glitz. She had her own shows on the radio when there was no television and movies were new. She was an extra in more than one of D.W. Griffith's films, and she was friends with Bebe Daniels and Harold Lloyd. She married Fred Patten in 1916 and had one daughter, Rae, my mother.

As I did in part one, I'm writing a few notes in brackets for clarity, but these are my grandmother's words.

Favorite sheet music and songs — early 1900s

Dad must have had the store longer than I realized. Mom would tell of me at two or three years old walking, rather toddling, between the hind legs of one of our horses while she and Dad held their breath. Then out the front legs I went. The horse never moved. That was a breath-taker, I imagine.

Dad had an oil house at the side of the store in front of the barns. He had tanks of coal oil as people bought that for farming machinery and lamps. Also gasoline. Dad was quite a drinker at one time, and he kept his booze, bottles of it, hidden around those oil tanks. I am pretty strong-willed, so one day, I went into the oil house and emptied out all his booze and filled the bottles with water. Wow, was Dad mad—but I wasn't punished.

Dad had a sweetheart, Jane Doe. Mom wasn't even jealous (she said). The townspeople disliked Jane. She wasn't a nice person, scandal, etc. She and Dad would go to Los Angeles on a binge or to the races at Arcadia. The train went right by the race track. I was never there, too young, but would see it from the train window as Mom and we kids would go to L.A. to visit Aunt Cora.

The townspeople would not allow Jane Doe in the church, and Mom was some lady. She said that was what churches were for. Good people didn't have to go to church. She finally got Jane into the Christian Church, but I don't think Jane was too crazy about it. During those times I think Mom was the boss of the store. The drummers (salesmen) liked her. Mr. Lunsford especially. A good-looking man.

I was only a kid, not even ten years old, and I remember all this. Dad had most of the grocery business in the valley, but everyone charged groceries then. No cash. It was rough collecting. I think Dad finally went bust.

Dad's coffee was in barrels, loose, and was dipped out with small hand shovels to weigh. The barrels were graded as cheaper coffee, better, and best. Of course, different prices. Dad used to say it was all the same coffee. The people didn't know the difference. Some just had to pay more.

I would make fudge candy once in a while and put it in our candy case and sell it. A young fellow (dandy type) would always buy most of it. He was in a higher grade than I, but I thought he was pretty nice. Don. Our candy case was at the front of the store. Dad used to say I lost all the profits on candy as I took candy to school and gave it to the kids. Our elementary school went to the eighth grade, but we moved to Ocean Park when I was passed from the seventh grade. I went to eighth at Ocean Park. [The family moved to Rose Avenue in Santa Monica, down the street from Charlie Chaplin and Harold Lloyd, in 1910.]

Now back to our house and store. We always had a game going at night in front of our store. The kids would congregate, choose sides, play hide-and-seek, and run sheep run, all over the main street. Sure had fun. We had many parties — birthdays, etc. Our friends all lived in orange groves, and we again would play those games. There was always a home base. We sure had fun around those orange trees. Hot-blooded young

Marvel Shepperd with her doll, c. 1906

kids. In the house, we played many kissing games. Post office, spin the bottle, all kissing games.

We were never afraid to go home in the dark. No street lights. No cars. No troubles. It was great.

Dad's customers the Beckwiths were very good friends of ours. Mrs. Beckwith and Mom, especially. They lived in an orange grove in the northern part of Glendora. They had two children, Charles and Dorothy. I stayed all night with them quite often, and we kids played doctor. Just kid stuff. So near, and yet so far. They were wealthy and had a lovely home. They had the first automobile in Glendora. What a thrill to ride in it for a few blocks to their house. That had to be around 1904 or 1905. I wish I had words to express the thrill of that car. I remember it was a limousine, a four-seater, high off the ground. I don't remember any windows or the name of it. You had to crank it. Not a Ford — had a high-class name.

The Beardslees, great friends of the De Shields family, owned a two-story home in an orange grove. They were of the wealthy class and also owned a house at Long Beach. Every summer we had our vacation at Long Beach in the Beardslee house on Magnolia. We kids slept on the floor. I wonder why.

Dad would buy our train ticket at the station. It was a thrill to see the train coming down the tracks and know we could go aboard. We would go past Azusa, Duarte, Monrovia, Arcadia, Pasadena, and arrive at the L.A. station that was near a bridge, maybe North Broadway or could be Seventh Street bridge, right where all the tracks were. No big stations yet. With a horse and buggy one had to drive over the bridge and down on the other side to the station. From there, we would get the train to Long Beach. It seems like we sat on side seats. Good times. Maybe they were tram cars, I'll bet.

Glendora was very hot in the summer. The Fourth of July was scorching. The winters were cold. It was so beautiful to see snow on Mount Baldy and many mountaintops and the golden oranges in the valley. Orange blossoms would scent the whole valley.

The first days of spring, Mom would let us take off our long underwear and shoes and go barefooted. The earth felt so good to our feet. We would take off our shoes on the way home from school. What joy!!

I used to walk in my sleep. One night Grandma was staying all night and sleeping in my room, and she caught me trying to get out the window. Grandpa would sing in his sleep. Ethel and I would be awakened and Grandpa was singing loud and clear. Not bad, either. It was strange because he was such a quiet man.

Ethel and Kenneth Kamphefner, c. 1902

Frank Shepperd's stepson Bill lost his leg in an Azusa rock quarry.

The Blunt kids lived near Kenneth, and he told me they would ring frogs through the wringer of the washing machine. They were mean little kids. [Kenneth Kamphefner's home was in Little Dalton Canyon where the debris basin is now. Before he died, Bill Cullen told me he spent a lot of time as a child in the Kamphefner home.]

Uncle Frank [Shepperd] used to break horses. He would have a horse or two, tie them to a pole, run them around and around in a ring, and he had a long leather whip he would use on them as he cussed and yelled. It made me sick. And yet he was fun, took us on picnics in the wagon drawn by two horses.

We used to walk towards the mountains up to Silent's Park. We ate oranges and tangerines on the way. That was the most charming rustic place I have ever been. Sort of terraced, irregular paths up and down, rustic seats, ferns, flowers, trees. We could hide and giggle at the boys.

We came home all tired out. It was at the base of the mountains, very hilly. I wonder if it is still there.

I forgot to mention Halloween. What a night. It wasn't so much door-to-door activity as it was the big kids out doing mischief. They'd dump over backhouses and leave a stinking, gaping hole. Uncle Henry had to put his toilet back over the hole every year. The kids would get buggies and put the privies on top of houses or stores. (There weren't many stores.) The next day everyone was out looking for them.

They had a soda fountain in the drugstore — a place for the kids to hang out. I liked pineapple ice cream sodas, five and ten cents, a big glass. Good.

I remember the San Francisco earthquake when S.F. was burned up. That was 1906, I think. [April 18, 1906.] Mom gathered up lots of clothing to send to the victims who were homeless, living in parks.

It was around that time, we were in school in the afternoon and it was almost time to go home. We heard the bells ringing all over town and that meant fire. So school out, excited kids started down the street towards home and could see the smoke. It was the house next to ours. People were bringing furniture out of our house, even the piano. They got everything out except some old pictures on the shelf of the clothes closet. I wish I had them. The fire soon took over our house. Someone had to stay at the store.

Anyway, we moved to the second story of the land office building across from our store near the old Glendora Hotel. Our furniture had been put under the trees across the street from the burning house. Of course, we couldn't do our acrobatics there anymore, but we still had the old hitching post bar in front of the store.

[The Glendora Land Office building was built on the southwest corner of Leadora and Vista Bonita when that was the center of town, but by the time Frances' family home burned, the town center had changed, and the Land Office had been moved to the northeast corner of Meda and Michigan (Glendora) Avenues. The Hotel Belleview was located almost next to it, between Michigan and Vista Bonita on the north side of Meda Avenue.]

Everyone had iceboxes. I wonder where the ice came from. It was delivered from an ice wagon. That's all I know. No electric washer and dryer like now. We washed clothes in a tub on a washboard by hand but had a wringer to put on the tub. We had a clothesline in the back yard. We did not cook in the office building after the fire. We cooked in the store.

Grandma helped us a lot as Mom was busy at the store. I don't remember how we got along in that office building. My piano was in a little alcove at the stairway, and that is where I practiced and had lessons from

Ada Whitaker's parents owned the Hotel Belleview. She was a pianist who played duets with Frances.

"Hello Central, Give Me Heaven" sheet music, 1901

the Pomona lady. Ada Whitaker, the daughter of the people who owned the hotel, took lessons from the same teacher, and we played recitals, double piano, duets at the hotel. Real nice. I was seven when Mom had been to L.A. and brought home "Oh, You Beautiful Doll" sheet music. That was the beginning of the end of my classical music.

I sang in church also. Mom played the organ. I still have the music, all patched up with tape, to this song I sang. "Hello Central Give Me Heaven 'Cause My Mother's There." It was among Mom's long-treasured music.

Grandma Shepperd was a revered and respected lady in Glendora. She was always ready to help when called on for the sick or poor. A very avid churchgoer. In fact, we all went to church on Sunday, and Sunday school and prayer meeting on Thursday night.

There was no dancing, no card playing in Glendora, ever. We still had lots of fun.

First I will tell of Grandpa. He had a severe sunstroke. I don't know when. It left him a little addled, and he would wander away on a long walk. Everyone knew about old Jake and someone would always bring him home. He would just walk and walk, and they would find him sitting under a tree. A gentle man. [Jacob Shepperd was blind and ill of sunstroke after the Civil War in Topeka, Kansas. He recovered his sight.]

Train trips to L.A.: Aunt Cora was exciting. She was not a pretty woman, was round-shouldered but sure had something, probably a personality. I was so young. We took the train to L.A. and got on a yellow streetcar that went out Temple Street. The old Natick Hotel was on Main Street in Los Angeles. That is where the City of Los Angeles was, just Main Street. Cora lived in a small yellow house, and there was quite a drop in back of her house. It was like a cliff with shrubs. She and Jim Campbell had Ivanilla, Don, and Ralph. We always had fun, but Mom always helped her out. She never had much money.

Sometimes Mom would send me alone to visit Aunt Cora. One time, she took me to the old Natick Hotel, the best, where we had dinner with a man. She had divorced Uncle Jim. I might have been eight or nine years old. We saw "The Girl of the Golden West," an old romantic western play on the stage. During a tragic scene, someone was killed upstairs in the playhouse, and blood dripped out of the ceiling. So they talk about violence now. 'Twas always thus. Cora didn't have to take me but enjoyed showing me the city. I was enthralled and wanted to be an actress.

She married twice after divorcing Uncle Jim and then married Uncle Jim at last again. Cora's younger son Don died in the big Long Beach earthquake. They lived in Compton, his wife also. He tried to turn the gas out under the house, and there was another shake that moved the house on top of him. It crushed him, and he died some months later. I don't know what happened to Ralph and Ivanilla.

Uncle Frank [Shepperd] had a flair up in his family. He took in a man boarder. Aunt Alice and the boarder fell in love. Aunt Alice took the girls and left with the man. They went up north around Fresno, and we never saw the girls until years later at the pioneer picnic. I missed Winifred, Marvel, and Jennie. We had had lots of fun at their house. I liked all of my cousins. Winifred was pretty. We all liked Aunt Alice.

Uncle Frank married twice after Aunt Alice. Aunt Addie had two girls and a son. The girls were Della and Dollie. The son was Bill. Uncle Frank adopted them. Della is still my friend. Dolly died early. She was in a sanitarium for dope. Bill had his leg cut off by a little car at the rock crusher, full of rocks. The rock crusher was between Azusa and Monrovia near the Santa Ana River. [The San Gabriel River.] That river came out of the mountains and runs clear to Huntington Beach. It is dry most of the time now, but when I was a child, that river would rage in the winter as we had lots of rain. The railroad bridge was across it, and the waters would wash out the bridge. Lots of excitement, believe me. Our wash emptied into the Santa Ana River. [The San Gabriel River.]

We don't have those rains any more, and the river bed is dry most of the time. The old wash has been gone for years.

Thoughts: I do remember. We had a telephone on the wall at the store, and Dad and Mom took orders for feed and groceries. I think only people who lived a little distance away had telephones in their homes. I don't remember when electric lights came in. We had to pull a string to turn them on. Same with toilets when they finally put them in the house. Pull the string to flush it. [Electricity was introduced in Glendora in April 1908, according to Donald Pflueger's *Glendora.*]

I must have been nine or ten when they had big electric cars running from Los Angeles to Glendora. That was a big day when the first car pulled up at the new station on the main street. Mom was the big leader for the celebration. She had a big feed at the station with help. What a big time that was. We were still living in the office building. [December 20, 1907.]

After thoughts: "I forget to remember." My folks had some friends in Pomona who had one child, a daughter. I can't remember the names, but I liked them a lot. Mom would put me on the train alone (what a thrill). The conductor would see that I got off at Pomona. They would meet me, and I would stay a week or whatever. We always had a lot of fun. It seems like a big deal was to go to the library. Sounds silly now. Her father was a barber and lots of fun. No automobiles or street cars. So walk.

Thoughts: Mom and speeches. Mom was always a student and participated in many activities. She took up oratory and made speeches for W.C.T.U. contests. I have four of her medals, one a diamond. She spoke for the Grand Diamond and lost. This was in Pomona. We were so disappointed. But I was six or seven years old, so it was very exciting.

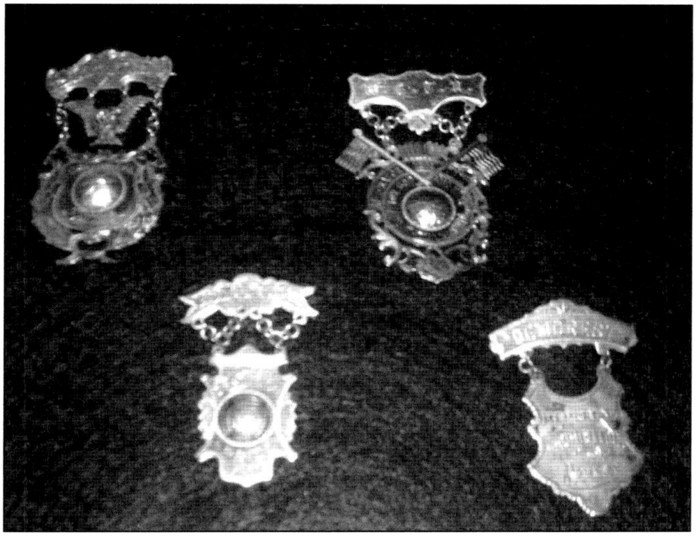

One silver and three gold medals that Maggie Shepperd won in Women's Christian Temperance Union speech contests founded by William Jennings Demorest who was a prohibition activist, c. 1900.

Mom did all the bookkeeping for the store. We had good friends, a milliner. Such beautiful hats she had in her own home. My mother had a big beauty with flowers, and my kid friends and I had our pictures taken in it. Her daughter was my girlfriend Ruby.

Another thought: Glen Odell [Glenn] was the owner of the bank in Glendora, and Glen my brother was named after him. [Glenn Odell started his dental practice in 1908 in an office above the De Shields' grocery store.]

I must mention this fun. Kenneth [Kamphefner] and I got an old wagon body with wheels and would haul it up the incline by their house, hang on ropes to steer the thing, and it would roll fast down that hill. Sure was fun. Orange groves and pepper trees on both sides of the road. We could have smashed into something but never did. I think my brothers were in on that and Ethel also.

Our school was fun. If we took our lunch, we girls would sit under a big spreading pepper tree, nice tall big green weeds underneath. When we finished and the bell rang, the weeds were mashed flat. The backhouse toilet was near there. Orange groves were across the street. The school was two stories, a frame building, just one building and wide, wide steps all across the front. We had a picture with Bob, Glen and me in it. I was near the top of the steps and Glen in the first row. The whole school on those steps. I wish I could find that picture. I was eight or nine. [Glendora Grammar School.]

Maybe I can get to Dad's folks now.

I loved my grandparents on both sides, paternal and maternal. Grandma was called Aunt Frank or Aunt Fanny by friends. [Katherine Frances Casey De Shields.] Grandpa was called De Shields. [William Jasper De Shields.] He had big whiskers. When he died, they were on top of the sheet. I noticed that. "Young thoughts." No, I don't know where they met. Grandpa and his family and ancestors came from France. Huguenots, he said. Grandpa was from Louisiana where they had settled. Grandma was born in Texas as a Casey. She had relatives in Pomona whom we used to visit. We were children, of course. They were Dad's cousins, I believe. Walter Casey was a renowned corporate lawyer in Los Angeles. His brother, Walter John Casey, I believe, was postmaster of Pomona for years and years. They were quite prominent people. An old lady, their grandma, I guess, smoked a pipe. They said she was a real French woman.

[William Jasper De Shields was born in Tennessee in 1838 to a family of French Huguenots, Protestants. Part of the family moved to Oregon in 1854, but after four months, William Jasper left them there to travel down to the Gold Rush near the Sutter mines. He settled in Glendora where he married John Casey's daughter Katherine Frances and homesteaded the land at the corner of Citrus and Gladstone. She had a brother named John Walter Casey, and she named one of her sons John Walter De Shields, Frances' father. The Casey who was postmaster of Pomona was probably John Walter Casey's son.]

Grandma used to tell us about coming from Texas to California in a covered wagon. The Indians scalped her cousin. This history is in books in the Azusa library. In fact, our family names are on a scroll with the events that happened to them being pioneers of the Azusa Valley, like Grandad's planting the first orange grove. [1874.] This scroll with the names of other pioneers is buried under a big rock in front of the Azusa Court House. The rock was brought down from the mountains. [The rock is still in front of Azusa City Hall.]

Grandpa and Grandma De Shields had six children. I don't know their ages. John Walter De Shields was my father. Uncle Robert (Bob) was an engineer on trains. Uncle Charlie married twice, to Aunt Lucy and Aunt Margaret. Uncle Louis lived in Fresno. Aunt Matt could have been the youngest. Aunt Emma married Joe Inman. He was quite a successful man, owned lots of land in Norwalk and was President of the Norwalk Bank. Uncle Joe and Aunt Emma had four children: Elliot, Emma, Fred, and I almost forgot Vivian. Vivian was so much older. She never was young, to me anyway, like Fred and Emma. Elliot died very young of consumption, they called it. Tuberculosis. [Vivian was Emma's child by a first marriage to Charles Miller who had died. His family owned the Glendora livery stable.]

Gladstone House. W.J. De Shields is the first name on the list of title deed owners of this house near Citrus and Gladstone, c. 2011.

Charles and Lucy De Shields, c. 1908

Maggie De Shields, a walking ad for California Fruit Gum, c. 1910

Aunt Matt, as I have written, lived at our house quite often, and she and Mom were good friends. Vivian also was a good friend of Mom's. Vivian was a school principal. Finally, after years in the Norwalk schools, she married a Norwalk man named Shaw and had two girls. One daughter was Bobbie Shaw. I don't remember much about Vivian after she married. Aunt Matt married a Fresno man and had a girl and boy. She and her husband eventually moved to San Diego, and we visited them. The boy was killed in a motorcycle accident while he was in the Navy. I didn't know them too well. Aunt Matt was a rough-and-ready woman. I liked her. Vivian was kind of prissy. Uncle Louis had a boy and girl. I did not know them. His boy was in the Navy and was killed during World War I. As I write, I think we have relatives all over the U.S. Can't keep them straight.

Uncle Bob I adored — handsome, jovial. Engineer on those big trains out of San Francisco. He had two handsome sons. I did not know his wife well. I send Xmas cards to the sons, both married and fathers, just continuing what Mom did. I have only met them once in Norwalk.

Uncle Charlie was also handsome and happy and gay. I was his favorite. He and Aunt Lucy had no children. When I was 5, 6, or 7, Mom let me visit them in Los Angeles. What fun. Uncle Charlie was driving a bakery wagon — not house to house. It must have been wholesale. Anyway, it was a horse and wagon, like a van. I remember crossing a bridge over the railroad tracks in L.A., and an automobile whizzed by and frightened us and the horse. I bet it was going twenty miles per hour. Funny days. Not many autos, that's for sure. I don't remember where their house was.

I loved Norwalk. We had a buggy that we hitched a horse to, but when we went to Norwalk, Mom and Dad would take a wagon with one horse. The big delivery wagon took two horses. Anyway, they'd make us three kids comfortable in the back. We could sleep if we felt like it, and we would drive to Norwalk. I would love to know the roads we took. I remember at one point, we went through a canyon that was beautiful, streams of water, etc.

Grandma and Grandpa [De Shields] always had a big feed for us, and we stayed with them. They had a cow and a horse named Bill and a buggy, of course, and they drove to Norwalk to shop.

They kept old Bill out in the field back of their house, and I loved to go with Grandad to get Bill and walk in the paths of salt grass, green and spongy. Barefooted, of course. I even learned how to hitch up a horse and milk a cow. I stayed with them by myself many times, and Grandma would hitch up Bill, and we would go visiting to Aunt Cary's in Carmenita, beautiful white home and barns and peacocks strutting around in the yards. We always had fun at Uncle Joe's and Aunt Emma's. They had everything — a huge barn where we could play in the haylofts. It was a long driveway from the street (Rosecrans, now) past the house, the windmill, to the barns. The windmill was on top of the silo. A silo is a tall, lean building where the corn grown for livestock was kept after harvesting. I loved to hear the windmill (like in Holland) going round and round and the same old clickity clack sound. We used to hide in the tall corn fields, and Aunt Emma would have us pick corn for dinner, with plenty of home-churned butter. Many times I have helped Grandma make butter. They didn't have refrigerators, and after milking, there would be many circular pans — stainless steel looked like — set out on the cool porch for the cream to set on top of the milk. Then it could be skimmed off to make butter. Fred and Emma and we kids liked to have a piece of homemade bread, skim off the thick cream, put it on the bread, and then sugar it. "Yumie-yum."

Joe had many many cows and lots of the milk was put into milk cans — big silver-looking cans — set in front of the house to be picked up and taken where they would prepare it to be sold in milk bottles, nothing plastic. There was a big huge pepper tree in back of the house — two orange trees by the silo. Uncle Joe bred horses also. When I would see a man bringing two big stud horses up the driveway to the barn, I wanted to run under the bed. I couldn't stand those squealing horses.

He had horses, lots of cattle, a bull, sheep. Fred would shear the sheep. A way out in the field, there was a swimming hole with tullies all around it. Tullies are tall, sort of like bamboo. We kids — Emma, Fred, Elliot, Bob, and I — would swim in that dirty big hole and it was fun. I wonder where the water came from.

They had fruit trees, and we would build mud houses under those trees and roads and tracks. Some fun. At the side of Grandma's house, I had a hopscotch game — just draw it with a stick and hop it.

Norwalk was sugar beet country. The boxcars of the train were always loading across the road from Uncle Joe's. Dad used to jack rabbit hunt every time we went to visit. Jack rabbits are good eating, but I never watched them skin the rabbits. Gads!!

Norwalk was all fields, farming, and cows. Sugar beets, corn, sugar cane. Everyone had a garden. I used to sell string beans, carrots, lettuce, etc. that Dad grew in Glendora to the neighborhood. A big bunch of anything for a nickel or dime.

Grandpa would take Grandma and I to La Mirada to visit someone. That was a pretty place. There was a railroad station there, very small, and there was one in Norwalk, just a train stop. It seems like after they put the trains in action that we took the train a few times. Someone would meet us with a horse-and-buggy. Carmenita, La Mirada, Los Alamitos, Artesia, Norwalk are all thriving towns now.

Uncle Joe's old homestead is still there, even the little house by the road where Grandad died. Emma's house on the other side is still there, even the cows. There, people have a dairy as did Fred after Uncle Joe died. Fred had a huge commercial dairy with the latest equipment and Swedes to take care of the milking machinery and cows.

Fred and Jennie [Inman] moved. They couldn't stand the houses being built, increased taxes, no more fields. They moved to Lake Elsinore. Emma II and her second husband live in Garden Grove. They are both wealthy, and Uncle Joe [Inman]

Frances and Fred Patten in Glendora foothills, c. 1916

owned nearly all of Norwalk and the land the Norwalk Mental Hospital is on. Sold now.

The folks would drive us to Los Alamitos to the beach. It was the closest one to Norwalk. Horse-and-buggy, of course.

To me, one of the most memorable times I remember is being barefooted and walking in paths. Wonderful footworn paths through green fields of wildflowers. Another thing was having all of our families together and the cousins. Dad's brothers and sisters all called Grandma just "Ma," likewise "Pa." They were a very close family, and I loved it.

In Glendora, all the streets were lined with trees, pepper, mostly. Orange groves everywhere, dirt roads. Frogs and crickets at night. Coyotes. Everyone had a dog or cats. Country life. No cars, no need to lock a door. Our store was so much fun. We knew everyone.

Giggling in church, always church and Sunday school. Mom, a "big frog in a little puddle," a stately, lovely loved woman just like her mother. Aunt Ollie [Kamphefner] like a little mouse. Uncle Henry, the boss. Aunt Ollie's word to describe any disaster was sh_t. So funny to hear her say it. She was so unassuming. Ethel [Kamphefner] sitting on the steps during recess and me racing around playing games — basketball, baseball. I always had a beau — whether they knew it or not. Notice all my little square pictures I have for you. They were taken at school I think, or else someone came to Glendora and the little towns taking pictures of the kids.

This is a summary of my story. I may think of more later. This is November 20, 1977.

Frances Rae Patten, c. 1941

Fred Patten, c. 1935

Epilogue

When I was writing my articles, I was taking watercolor classes at Citrus College from Chris Van Winkle. He was an extraordinary artist and a fine teacher. One day critiquing my painting and reinforcing the first rule — not to paint the whites — he said, "Layne, you paint the shadows. God paints the light." He believed each work was a record of the movement of light across a subject. I find this to be true of writing history. A writer can record only the sensory information he can find about the past and has to rely on imagination to shed light on his vision.

Our ancestors were able to sit on a porch in the San Gabriel Valley in the early evening and smell orange blossoms on trees in their orchards, but which of us has the imaginative power to smell citrus as we read about the growth of that industry? We may envision the beauty of sunsets and sunrises that stretched into infinity on a clear day in the 1800s, but our imaginative power struggles to remove the urban skyline of wires and high-rises that make the horizon an illusory line now. The emotional layer of history is often lost in the writing of it. I've admitted to speculating about the past, but I included my grandmother's memoirs because the immediacy of childhood memories makes her version of Glendora's history tangible. Her "oh, yeah!" and "what joy!" and "gads!" make life around 1900 real. You can feel the shock of seeing a baby — your own — toddle lengthwise beneath a tethered horse and know the surprise of suddenly hanging upside down by your knees in an outhouse. Yes, that misstep would ruin lunch, as she writes.

There are stories I couldn't include because I don't remember my sources or because they were snippets: A school teacher and her students were once terrified when a horse thief barged into their Glendora classroom, leaving his crew outside with the horses. The culprits were en route to their hideout in the foothills above Pasadena and were hungry, so they stole the children's lunches. The first bank robbery was unsuccessful; the dynamite shattered windows but didn't touch the vault. One pioneer slept in a shed for several years before he realized his mattress was on top of crates of dynamite. Oranges were shipped as far away as Japan in the 1870s. There was the wonder, too, of seeing the first trains run through the valley, the first cars kick up dust on unpaved roads, and the joy of talking on the first telephones.

Writing this book has enabled me to add some domesticity to the stories of town building and development. The early landowners had wives and children. In his mid-forties, Dalton converted to Catholicism and married Maria Guadalupe Zamorano who was only fourteen. They had eleven children, seven who survived. His homestead would have been a lively place atop an Azusa hill even without the workers he hired. He paid men to work in his orchards, fields, vineyard, tannery, stables, and granaries, and those men had families. His adobe homestead was a small community including whites, Mexicans, and Indians whose children attended the same adobe school with the settlers' children. To think of Dalton as only a businessman and litigant reduces the richness of his life on the Rancho Azusa. It was a western life. At one point in the 1840s, Indians stole his herd of horses and hid them in the foothills where they were later found and returned, and there were cattle drives. He and his son protected their water ditch with pistols, and the family's religious services were held at the secularized and declining San Gabriel Mission. To reach the church was a Sunday outing behind a horse and cart. I can only hint at the flurry of activity that was the past.

Of course, you learn about yourself and your lifestyle every time you write, but when you write history, your values are clarified. To be lucky enough to have interested friends and relatives share in your observations is a blessing. My friend Linda Colley has cast light on many thoughts in this book. It was she who noticed the absence of small electrical appliances among the wedding gifts in one photograph. She also suggested that not everyone enjoys a leisurely walk around a cemetery looking at headstones. Point taken. And isn't my great-grandmother's recipe for corn cakes perhaps the predecessor of our corn dog?

I've found my lost loved ones over and over again as I've written these pages. I count my blessings that their values and camaraderie have been passed down to me through generations, and I'm hoping others, especially my living family members, will enjoy knowing the journey across land and through time that has brought us to the present.

Thank you for sharing this trip with me.

Endnotes

Family records are the basis for these articles. Because the style of the *Glendoran* magazine did not require footnotes, some bits of information can't be credited now. Most sources are cited either as quotations or attributions within each chapter, and information about commonly known events, like the Civil War, is easily accessible both in libraries and on the internet. Research was done to provide an historical context, not to modify or revise the larger stories. The n.p. note indicates a work that has not been published.

Homesteaders

1. *Azusa Herald and Pomotropic, Commemorative Edition,* October 20, 1937.
2. *Azusa Pomotropic, Special Edition,* April 1894, Azusa Historical Museum, 1.
3. W. Wesley Kloepfer, "Azusa–The First 100 Years," (manuscript, Azusa City Library, 2001), 20-21, n.p.
4. Katherine Frances Casey, "Recollections of Covered Wagon Days from Texas to California," (memoir, Layne Staral Collection), n.p.
5. Reta De Shields Parton, emails to Layne Staral, October–November 2006; "De Shields Family History and Related Families, as of October 1, 1999," (manuscript, Layne Staral Collection) n.p.
6. Sheldon G. Jackson, *A British Ranchero in Old California: The Life and Times of Henry Dalton and the Rancho Azusa,* 179–188.
7. Jackson, 105-106.
8. Kloepfer, 221.
9. Kloepfer, 102-103, letter XXVII.
10. Casey, "Recollections."

11. Kloepfer, 21.

12. Jackson, 208-209.

13. "Minutes of the Proceedings of the Board of Water Commissioners San José and Azusa Townships, 1871-1878," (manuscript, Glendora Historical Museum) n.p.

14. Donald Pflueger, *Glendora: The Annals of a Southern California Community,* 200-201.

15. *An Illustrated History of Los Angeles County, California,* (Chicago: The Lewis Publishing Company, 1889), John Casey, 719-720, John W. Casey, 720.

16. Casey, "Recollections."

17. Bobbie Battler, "De Shields Land," The *Glendoran* magazine*,* January–February 1989, 72; *Title Search Report,* Maria and Alejandro Ornelas Collection. (See Appendix.)

18. Darell Clark, emails to Layne Staral, 2006; Ancestry.com, email Susan Morris McGee to Layne Staral, 2006.

19. Polley Dougherty, "Annual Minutes of the Old Settlers Association of the East San Gabriel Valley," (manuscript, Azusa Historical Museum,) n.p.

The Oregon Whitcombs

1. Whitcomb, "Memories From a Sunny Glen," (newspaper clipping, Glendora Historical Museum), 20–21.

2. Pflueger, *Glendora*, 35-38.

3. Pflueger, 27-28.

4. Historical Census Racial/Ethnic Numbers in Los Angeles County, 1850–1980, web.

5. Pflueger, 26.

6. De Shields, Maggie, "Letter to Paul Keiser." (See Appendix).

7. Helen Kennard Bettin, *This I Remember*, 138.

8. See abbreviated family trees in the Appendix.

9. De Shields, Letter. (See Appendix).

10. Roy Elliott, *Profiles of Progress, Sweet Home: The Story of Early Events and Pioneer Families of Linn County*, 172.

11. Elliott, 171–174.

12. Martha Steinbacher, "Whitcomb Family."

13. *Lebanon Express Newspaper*, "Early Day Logging."

1895 Linking Pioneer Genes

1. Minutes: Glendora Historical Society, March 28, 1949, Mrs. De Shields, 4. Maggie De Shields said at this meeting, "My folks lived in what was called the Bradley House." She said nothing more about the house.
2. Bobbie Battler, "De Shields Land," The *Glendoran* magazine, January–February 1989, 72; Title Search Report, Maria and Alejandro Ornelas Collection. (See Appendix.)
3. Jennie Porter Shepperd to daughter Meda Ella Shepperd Whitcomb, December 4, 1905, Layne Staral Collection, letters to Meda Ella Shepperd Whitcomb 1899–1924.
4. Frances P. De Shields, (memoir, Layne Staral Collection), 1987, no pagination.
5. Pflueger, *Glendora* 52.
6. Maggie Shepperd De Shields, 1956 taped interview for the Old Settlers of the East San Gabriel Valley organization on CD #3, Track 2, 3:30, Glendora Historical Museum.
7. De Shields, memoir.
8. Pflueger, 56.
9. Peck, M. Scott, M.D., *In Search of Stones,* (New York: Hyperion, 1995), 117.
10. Maggie De Shields to her sister Meda, January 9, 1909, Layne Staral Collection, letters to Meda Ella Shepperd Whitcomb,1899–1924.

The Cullen Legacy

An interview with the late Bill Cullen II in 2008 is the primary source of information for this chapter. His daughter Karen Cullen and her husband Dan Wilshire clarified and expanded some parts of the family history and provided digitized photographs. They also shared a cassette tape dated 6/19/94 of Bill Cullen telling his life story.

From the Civil War to Glendora

Please see the Works Cited for source material.

The Clardy-Engelhardt Legacy

The Engelhardt family album was crammed with clippings, documents, pictures, and memorabilia from this family history when the late Bob Hillman lent me the book for my 2009 article. I have no access to it now.

Glendora's Water Dowser

Marquita Shepperd Barber shared her family records in 2010, and I've enjoyed a second and recent telephone conversation with Rob Thompson whose website — robthompsondowsing.com — explains more about water dowsing than I can.

Works Cited

Homesteaders

I. UNPUBLISHED WORKS

Battler, Bobbie. "De Shields Land." The *Glendoran* magazine. Jan-Feb 1989.

Clark, Darell. Emails to Layne Staral, 2006.

De Shields, Katherine Frances Casey. "Recollections of Covered Wagon Days from Texas to California." Layne Staral Collection.

Dougherty, Polley. "Annual Minutes of the Old Settlers Association of the East San Gabriel Valley." Manuscript. Azusa Historical Museum.

Kloepfer, W. Wesley. "East San Gabriel Valley's Earliest Pioneers – Post Indian Era (1780-1910)." Manuscript. 2000. Azusa City Library.

Kloepfer, W. Wesley. "Azusa–The First 100 Years." Manuscript. 2001. Azusa City Library.

McGee, Susan Morris. Email to Layne Staral. 2006.

"Minutes of the Proceedings of the Board of Water Commissioners San José and Azusa Townships, 1871-1878." Ledger. Glendora Historical Museum.

Parton, Reta De Shields. "De Shields Family History and Related Families, as of October 1, 1999." Manuscript. Layne Staral Collection.

Taggart, Sarah Ellen. "Oakland Woman Born in Texas as Conflict Raged; Wagon Train Ambushed." "Covered Wagon Baby Dies In Oakland Home." Layne Staral Collection. 1937.

II. PUBLISHED WORKS

An Illustrated History of Los Angeles County, California. Chicago: The Lewis Publishing Company, 1889. Web: Library of Congress. Casey, 719-720.

Azusa Pomotropic, Special Edition. April 1894: 1.

Azusa Herald and Pomotropic, Commemorative Edition. October 20, 1937: 1.

Fracasse, Ida and Joe. The *Glendoran* magazine. Glendora: Liberty Enterprises, 1983–2023.

Jackson, Sheldon G. *A British Ranchero in Old California: The Life and Times of Henry Dalton and the Rancho Azusa.* Glendale: Arthur H. Clark Company, 1987.

Pflueger, Donald. *Glendora: The Annals of a Southern California Community.* Claremont: Saunders Press, 1951.

Woolsey, Ronald C. *Migrants West: Towards the Southern California Frontier.* Sebastopol: Grizzly Bear Publishing Company, 1996.

The Oregon Whitcombs

I. UNPUBLISHED WORKS

De Shields, Maggie. Letter to Paul Keiser, undated. (See Appendix.)

Steinbacher, Martha. "Whitcomb Family." Photocopy of a handwritten article. Sweet Home Genealogical Society, Oregon.

II. PUBLISHED WORKS

Bettin, Helen Kennard. *This I Remember.* City of Industry: Zephyr Publications, 1990.

Elliott, Roy A. *Profiles of Progress, Sweet Home: The Story of Early Events and Pioneer Families of Linn County.* Eugene, Oregon, 1971.

Lebanon Express Newspaper. "Early Day Logging Dependent on Nature, Man's Ingenuity." July 14, 1965. Photocopy.

Whitcomb, Charles and Theresa. "Memories From a Sunny Glen." The Glendora *Signal*. July 27, 1989: 20-21.

1895 Linking Pioneer Genes

I. UNPUBLISHED WORKS

De Shields, Maggie Shepperd. 1956 taped interview for the Settlers of the East San Gabriel Valley on CD #3, Track 2. Glendora Historical Museum.

De Shields, Maggie. Letter to sister Meda Ella Whitcomb. Jan 9, 1909. Layne Staral Collection.

Glendora Historical Society. Minutes. March 28, 1949.

Ornelas, Maria and Alejandro. Gladstone House, Title Search Report. (See Appendix.)

Shepperd, Jennie Porter. Letter to daughter Meda Ella Shepperd Whitcomb. December 4, 1905. Layne Staral Collection.

II. PUBLISHED WORKS

Battler, Bobbie. “De Shields Land.” The *Glendoran* magazine, Jan–Feb 1989.

Peck, M. Scott, M.D. *In Search of Stones.* New York: Hyperion,1995.

From the Civil War to Glendora

Fehrenbacher, Don E. *Prelude to Greatness: Lincoln in the 1850's.* Stanford, California: Stanford University Press, 1962.

Goodwin, Doris Kearns. *Team of Rivals: The Political Genius of Abraham Lincoln.* New York: Simon and Schuster, 2005.

Oates, Stephen B. *The Approaching Fury: Voices of the storm, 1820-1861*. New York: Harper Collins, 1997.

Pflueger, Donald. *Glendora: The Annals of a Southern California Community*. Claremont, California: Saunders Press, 1951.

Randall, J.G. and David Donald. *The Civil War and Reconstruction.* Boston: D.C. Heath and Company, 1961.

Stratton, Joanna L. *Pioneer Women: Voices from the Kansas Frontier*. New York: Simon and Schuster, 1981.

Swanson, James L. *Manhunt: The 12-Day Chase for Lincoln's Killer*. New York: Harper Collins, 2006.

The Clardy-Engelhardt Legacy

Battler, Bobbie. "Engelhardt Family Developed Homes, Business." Highlander-Publications, December 26, 1984, A-2.

Battler, Bobbie. "Downtown in the Early Years." The *Glendoran* magazine, Jan/Feb 1987, 54.

Guinn, James Miller. *Historical and Biographical Record of Los Angeles and Vicinity,* 1901. Web.

Kimball, Ruth Pratt. *Glendora History and Souvenir Program of the Golden Get-together Celebration,* May 29, 1937. Glendora: The Glendora Press-Gleaner. 1937.

Kobzeff, Mildred. "Pioneer Families Reunion." The *Glendoran* magazine. Jul/Aug 1996, 68–69.

A. Appendix
List of Members
SETTLERS OF THE EAST SAN GABRIEL VALLEY

The secretary's ledger contains references to mailing and membership lists that no longer exist. But it also contains necrology reports and references to officers, speakers, committee members, and other people who were involved in the activities of the picnic organization. All these have been noted to compile the following list of three or four generations of the earliest Azusa Valley settlers.

Abbott,
  Austen
  Alice Clark
Abdelnour, George
Ackerman,
  Clara La Fetra
  Preston
Adair, Janet
Aguilar, Tony
Akard, Bryan
Alva, Joe
Appe, Mrs. Phoebe
Arnold, Floyd
Austin,
  Sarah
  Winifred Jeffrey
Ayers, Mrs. Clara
Baker,
  Winnifred Brunjes
  Bertha
  Mrs. Horace G.
    (Abbie)
Barnes
Beardslee,
  Arthur
  Josephine
Behrens, Richard
Belcher,
  Mina
  Major
Bell, Dr. George
Bender,
  Mrs. Elbert
  John
  Aileen
Berheyen,
  Mildred Lang
Bernhardt, Ella
Bidwell,
  R.B.
  Ralph
Blackwood, Gordon
Blake, Phillip
Blatchley,
  H. L.
  Miriam
Bliss, Wallace
Blomgren, William
Boone, Ira
Boselly, Mrs. Harriett
Boudinot, Nolis
Bouldin, Myrtle Rench
Bradley, Bess
Bradshaw,
  Betty
  Claire
Brecht, Paul
Briggs, Dwight
Brittingham,
  Dona Harrin
Brockway, Joseph H.
Brokaw, Ola
Brown,
  Arthur and Mrs.
  Grace Fuller
Brunjes,
  Dick
  Mrs. Hilda
  Emma
  Metta
Carpenter, Charles
Carr, Charles W.
Carter, Gladys
  Loomis
Casey, Irene La
  Fetra
Casey, Mrs.
  Catherine
  [Two Casey families]

Casper,
William J.
Essie
Chamberlain,
Mrs. Mabelle
Donald
Chambers, Ed
Chester, Harry
Clapp, Charles F.
Coats, Jesse
Coffman,
Charles
Ed
Mae
Cook,
Dr. E.D.
Bailey
Cove, Jack
Crabtree, Lawrence
Crawford, Mary Lou
Crowell,
Birdie
Oscar
Cullen,
Gerald
Kathleen
Parkinson
Walter
May Engelhardt
Currier, Roy
Curry, C.D.
Curtis, Carrie
Daffurn, Charles
Dalton, Ottie
Dameral, Harry
Daniels,
Edna
Mrs. P.C.
Davies,
Will
Mrs. David
Davis, Glen
Dawford, Melissa C.
Dawson, Robert
De Shields,
Maggie (d. 5/30/71)
Charles Francis
Glen
Dodsworth, Dr.
Domer, George
Doss, Ann Clark
Dougherty,
Polly
Emmet
Drendel, William
Durrell, Judge J.O.
Easley,
Leonora
Bohannon
Virgil
Homer
Carl
Ebersoll, Leo
Ellington, George
Engelhardt,
Ernest
Clayton
Erna (Clayton)
Ernsberger,
Dr. George
Evans,
W.J.
Mrs. W.J.
Fay,
Dan
Mrs. Alma
Ferghson, Mrs. Grace
Foss, Allan
Frazier,
Ola White
Ben
Fridley, Charles
Fuhr, Anita Ward
Funk, Mary
Gabel, Eva Cass
Gable,
William
Arthur
Gajalva, Victor
Garnett, Calloway
Garrett,
George
Minnie
Gaulden, Charles
Gauldin,
Clara Frances
Jennie Hanes
Lucille
Gillenwater, Ethridge
Gipp, Emile
Glover, Ed
Goalby, Carrie
Goff, Virginia
Goodson, Bessie
Gordon,
J.T.
Dorothy, Mrs. Ross
Mrs. Charles
Edna, Mrs.
Wallace
Charles
Wallace
Gossard, Roy
Gowens, Lottie
Grant, Ralph
Granville, William
Gray, Herman
Green, Mrs. H.A.
Greninger, Helena
Griffiths,
Charles and Olive
Groninger, C.F. Curley
Hall, W.G.
Hanes,
William
Simeon
Hapre,
William Cumming
Hardesty, Ruth Yount
Harding,
Mrs. William Sr.
Major
Harkis, Verne
Harmmer, Ole
Haskell,
Mrs. Iowa
Floyd
Frances
Hassheider, Metta
Hastie, Mrs. Nell
Hayden, Ann,
Mrs. Floyd
Hefner, Henry
Hendrick,

E. Harry
Betty J.
Hengood, Minnie
Hennington, Mary
Hertenstein,
Reuben
Wesley
Heth,
Fred
Mrs. Valetta
T.F.
Verne
Hibsch,
Alba
John
Hodge, Victor
Hodson
Holcomb, Clyde
Holmes, Horace
Hopper,
Pearle
Bessie Matney
Horton, Ed
Howard,
Charles
Mrs. Charles
(Minnie)
Huges, Paul
Hulbirt, Dr. Ray
Humphrey,
Carl
Anna
Hutchinson, Louisa
Inman,
Emma De Shields
Jackson,
Andrew
Percy
Jameson, Mary Gard
Jamieson, Tom
Jamison, Wylie
Jamper, Helen Raney
Janes, Sue
Jeffery, Helen
Johnson,
Mrs. Walter
Walter
Johnston, Morris L.
Jones,
Mrs. Maurice
Laura Durrell
Earl
Ollie
John Jr.
Josep
Juden,
Charlotte Ann
(Scott)
Clara Mae
Kamphefner, George
Kauffman Family
Keim, Mattie
Kelsaw, Helen Jeffrey
Kendall, Frank
Kesperek, Adolph
Kimbrell, Elena Agilar
Klefinger, Nellie
Kuebury, Belle
Skidmore
Kuffel, Carl
Kuhn,
Ira
Mary
La Fetra, C.M.
Lane, Clyde
Lee,
Arleigh
Jim
Lewis,
Ina Reeves
Mrs. Joe
Mack
Joe
Arline
Blennerhasett
Logan, Alice
Long, Mrs. Fred
(Eula)
Loomis, Mr. & Mrs.
Loose, Harold
Lopez, Maria Trujillo
Love,
Addie
George
Lyman,
Ledora
Lloyd
Lyon, John
MacKay, Anita
Maeding, Ernest
Malone,
Everett
Dick
Mrs. Everett
Lonnie
Manning, Minnie
Matheson,
John
Ethel
Matney, Mrs. Bessie
Maxfield, Belle
Mayme
McCaslin, Walter
McCroarty,
John Steven
McCutchen, Chester
McDonald, Mrs. L.G.
McKee, William
McKenzie, Hector
Meecham, Norman
Meier,
Alvana Lepley
George
Charles (Tiny)
Gus
Memmesheimer,
Louie
Menard, Louise
Merritt, Hazel Eldred
Midkiff, Claud
Millar, Marguerite
Miller,
Estelle
Helen
Judge Al
Will
Tom
Monroe, Ida M.
Moody, George
Moon,
Charles

Ira
William
Moore,
Fred
Russell
Morgan,
Everett
Charley
Mabel
Mowers, Tansie
Granville
Muehe, Frances,
Mrs. Joe
Muench, Minnie
Mull, Dorothy
Comstock
Munson, Mrs.
Estella
Musser, Mabel
Myers, Myrtle
Nasser, Lee
Netzley,
Bert
Leonard
Newman, Henrietta
Nichols, Mabel Hoag
Nickle, Harold
Norcross,
Charles
Effie
Odell,
Glenn
Mrs.
Ogilvie, Rufus
Orndorff, Ella M.
Ott, George
Owen,
Mary Metcalf
A.G.
Parkinson,
Mr.
H.F.
James
Fenton
Peck,
Kate Heaton
Sedley
Gregory
Alonzo
Pettijohn,
Maria Wick
Edith
Peyton, Kirby
Pfleuger, Mrs. George
Pierce,
Irene Barnes
Morgan
Plemons, Harvey
Poage,
Leland
Carolyn
Pollard,
Harriett Elizabeth
Potter, Hazel
Preston,
Jim
J.C.
Mrs. H.
Quick,
Vivian
Eugene
Rankin, Eddie
Rasmussen, Harry
Reed,
Fannie Hanes
James A.
Roland
J.M.
Reiff, Floyd
Remaley,
William
Mrs. Tillie
Renaker, Leslie
Reynard, Etta
Cullen
Richardson,
Hagel Clark
Bert
Richter, Carl
Roberts, Jim
Robertson, Ernest
Robinson,
John
Bob
Rogers, Helen
Rounds, Marvin
Rucker, Clifford
Rury,
Will
Christine
Savage, Chester
Schott, Jake
Scofield, Della F.
Sellers, Darrow
Shaw, Vivian Miller
Sheldon, Edna,
Mrs. W.A.
Shoemaker,
C.B.
Mary
Shorey, Harry
Shuck, Leslie
Siddall, Hallim
Siemers, Bertha
Singleton, Mrs.
Elizabeth
Sitton, Johnny
Skidmore,
Jack
Steve
Smith,
Cornelius
Mrs. Cornelius
Conway
Leslie
Mrs. Leslie
Edgar
Guy
Eliza and Thomas
Mrs. Guy
Mrs. Wesley
Ollie (Mrs. Fred)
Henry J.
Mrs. Edgar (Erma)
Wesley
Snavely
Southerland,
Mr. Earl
Mrs. Earl

B. Appendix

UNDATED LETTER FROM MAGGIE DE SHIELDS TO PAUL KEISER, GLENDORA, c. 1930

Dear Paul:

The reason for the delay in writing to you is – I have the account of my sisters death, a paper clipping from Lebanon and have been looking for it so that I might get the date when she and her husband George Bennet Whitcomb, came from Kansas to Glendora, but I have failed to find it so thot I better write any way and tell you what I know of my people coming to Glendora.

My sister Meda Ella, her husband George B. Whitcomb and their son Geo. Ernest Whitcomb came a year or so ahead of my parents. Geo. B. worked with his father Geo. D., in Glendora's early days, contracting and building houses. Meda Ave was named for my sister. According to information received from the public library in Los Angeles, the name is an Indian word and means "a secret religious society." Another child was born to Geo. and Ella in Glendora – a boy Walter. When they left Glendora they went to Oregon and settled in the mountains in the vicinity of Sweet Home. At that time the only way to get to their place was on horseback. They were 30 miles from the nearest town. At that place two girls were born to them. When the girls were about 5 & 6 years old the two of them and Walter, over a short period of 3 weeks died of diphtheria and were burried there in the mountains. The remaining boy attended college at Corvallis, Oregon and became a Civil Engineer. He has lived for years in Lebanon, where he raised his family of two girls and one boy, Walter, who was in world war 1 and like many others was never well after the war was over and soon passed on. Ernest and his very fine wife still live in Lebanon in the house where my sister Ella spent her last days. Ernest has, for 10 or 12 years been employed by the city of Lebanon in the capacity of his trade.

My parents, Jacob Russell and Jennie Porter Shepperd, arrived in Glendora with three girls, Olive, Cora and myself, and son Frank on Dec. 2, 1887. We youngsters attended school in the old school building (which of course, was new at that time) Mr. Sykes was teaching at that time. I believe our next teacher was Prof. Eden who, with his wife lived in my sister Ella's house, on the street the school house is on. Mrs. Eden was organist at the Methodist church while they lived in Glendora. I recieved musical instruction from Mrs. Eden – my first teacher of music was Lulu Disbrow, my lessons were on the organ and washed dishes for John and Edith Jeffery for 25¢ per week and paid for my lessons. John published the Glendora paper at that time. My next teacher was Ada Whitcomb, Carl Whitcomb's first wife.

If any of this is of interest to any one, fine and dandy, if not – well every one has waste paper baskets.

Have sent letter to Ernest Washburn.

My very best to you and your family -

Mrs. M. De Shields
3236 Casitas Ave.,
LA 39, Ca.

Note: Ada Bradley Whitcomb was Carroll Whitcomb's wife.

C. Appendix

GLADSTONE HOUSE
TITLE SEARCH REPORT

Courtesy of Maria and Alejandro Ornelas

I. Homesteaded by Wm. DeShields - March 24, 1878

II. William DeShields and Catherine DeShields
to James L. Dougherty
25 acres -- $1050, September 10, 1883

III. James L. Dougherty
to Gladstone Improvement Company
23 Acres -- $7500, June 2, 1887

IV. Gladstone Improvement Company
to James L. Dougherty
Default on loan, April 10, 1889

V. James L. Dougherty
to Willis Ormiston
22 acres -- $5000, September 30, 1889

VI. W. Ormiston -- Deceased, April, 1903
to Azusa Valley Bank -- to settle estate
22 acres -- $3000, October 18, 1905

VII. Azusa Valley Bank -- P.C. Daniels, President
to Wm. Warren
20.95 Acres, 1911

VIII. Wm Warren and James B. Warren
to Iral Roller, 1943

IX. Iral Roller
to Edward and Mary Chollar, 1962

X. Edward and Mary Chollar
to Dennis King
1978, $88.000

Family Trees

These branches from family trees are included only as aids to reading. They were created from family records and checked against online public records and Ancestry.com to verify dates.

Casey Family	1st GENERATION Child, birth/Spouse/ Parents	2nd GENERATION Child, birth/Spouse/ Parents
Casey, John 1810/Sarah Nixon Thornburg	John Walter, 1840/Martha J. Boswell/John & Sarah	Mary Nixon, 1875/ **Clugston**/John W.& Martha
		Lorena Frances, 1878/ **Civella**/John W. & Martha
		John Ransome, 1882/?/ John W. & Martha
		Walter Tivus, 1885/?/John W. & Martha
	Sarah Ellen, 1847/James W. **Taggart**/John & Sarah	Lewis, 1849/?/James W. & Hannah Newkirk
		Sarah Jane, 1865/?/James W. & Sarah
		Mary Frances, 1867/?/ James W. & Sarah
		Anne, 1869/?/James W. & Sarah
		Elizabeth, 1871/?/James W. & Sarah
		James Cecil, 1874/?/ James W. & Sarah
		John Turpin, 1877/?/James W. & Sarah

Casey Family	1st GENERATION Child, birth/Spouse/ Parents	2nd GENERATION Child, birth/Spouse/ Parents
		Wesford, 1879/?/James W. & Sarah
		Dora Melvina Ann, 1882/?/ James W. & Sarah
		Martha Belle, 1884/?/ James W. & Sarah
		Alice May, 1887/?/James W. & Sarah
	Katherine Frances, 1850/W.J. **De Shields**/ John & Sarah	Emma Alice, 1867/Charles **Miller**/Joseph W. **Inman**/ Katherine & W. J.
		John Walter, 1875/Mary Margaret Shepperd/ Katherine & W.J.
		Charles Francis, 1878/?/ Katherine & W.J.
		Louis Martin, 1880/?/ Katherine & W.J.
		Robert Casey, 1882/?/ Katherine & W.J.
		Mattye/?/Katherine & W.J.

Cullen Family	1st GENERATION Child, birth/Spouse/ Parents	2nd GENERATION Child, birth/Spouse/ Parents	3rd GENERATION Child, birth/Spouse/ Parents
Cullen, William Bryant, 1841/Mary Alice Fitzgerald	Mary Maud, 1871/ none/William & Mary		
	John Walter, 1873/ May Engelhardt/ William & Mary	Richard Henry, 1913/none/John W. & May	
		John, 1913/none/ John W. & May	
		May Catherine, 1915/**Roll**/John W. & May	
		William Bryant, 1921/Marion Edith Crain/John W. & May	Pam, ?/ **Rodewald**/ Bill & Marion
			Karen, ?/Dan **Wilshire**/Bill & Marion
			William, ?/none/ Bill & Marion
			John, ?/none/Bill & Marion
	Etta Mae, 1876/**Reynard**/ William & Mary		
	Margaret, 1880/Bert **Roll**/ William & Mary		
	Clara Bell, 1882/John **Rieker**/ William & Mary		
	William Gerald, 1885/Sue Nichols Sutherland/William & Mary		
	Agnes Harriet, 1887/Engbert **Van der Sluis**/ William & Mary		
	Edward Owen, 1890/none/William & Mary		

Engelhardt Family	1st GENERATION Child, birth/Spouse/ Parents	2nd GENERATION Child, birth/Spouse/ Parents
Engelhardt, Heinrich "Henry" David, 1814/Anna Maria Diehl	Henry David, 1845/ Katherine Kamphefner/Henry & Anna	Anna Mary, 1870/ **Stower**/Henry D. & Katherine
		John Gracen, 1874/ died/Henry D. & Katherine
		Clara Bell, 1875/ **Rietzke**/Henry D. & Katherine
		Nellie May, 1877/**Cullen**/Henry D. & Katherine
		August "Gusty" E., 1886/died/Henry D. & Katherine
		Jesse T., adopted 1893/?/Henry D. & Katherine
	John Peter, 1849/ Rose Hesse/Henry & Anna	Orton Hesse [**Englehart**],1900/?/ John P. & Rose
	George H., 1851/?/ Henry & Anna	
	Rose, 1853/?/Henry & Anna	
	August E., 1857/Rosa Clardy/ Henry & Anna	Clayton, 1889/?/ August & Rosa
		Ernest, 1890/?/ August & Rosa
		Walter, 1892/?/ August & Rosa

Shepperd Family	1st GENERATION Child, birth/Spouse/ Parents	2nd GENERATION Child, birth/Spouse/ Parents
Shepperd, Jacob Russell 1836, Jennie Collins	Letticia Olive, 1863/ died 1863/Jacob & Jennie	
	William Russell, 1864/Alice May Kammerdiener/ Jacob & Jennie	Juanita, 1905/?/ William & Alice
		Waldo Russell, 1907/?/William & Alice
		Freda Ynez, 1911/?/ William & Alice
		Arlone Ramona, 1914/?/William & Alice
	Meda Ella, 1866/George Bennett **Whitcomb**/Jacob & Jennie	George Ernest, 1886/Hazel Gwinn/ Meda & George Bennett
		Walter Roland, 1888/died 1899/ Meda & George Bennett
		Arella, 1892/died 1899/Meda & George Bennett
		Leadora, 1893/ died 1899/Meda & George Bennett
	Frank Howard, 1871/Alice M. Chadwick/Adeline Knuedeler/Jacob & Jennie	Alice M., 1891/?/ Frank & Alice
		Winifred Alice, 1896/?/Frank & Alice

Shepperd Family	1st GENERATION Child, birth/Spouse/ Parents	2nd GENERATION Child, birth/Spouse/ Parents
		Marvel Anita, 1899/?/Frank & Alice
		Jennie Marie, 1900/?/Frank & Alice
	Olive Elizabeth, 1873/Henry **Kamphefner**/Jacob & Jennie	Ethel R., 1894/?/ Henry & Olive
		Kenneth, 1897/?/ Henry & Olive
		Vernon, 1907/?/ Henry & Olive
	Mary Margaret, "Maggie" 1875/John Walter **De Shields**/ Jacob & Jennie	Frances Porter, 1896/Fred Patten/ Maggie & Walter
		Robert William, 1897/Marguerite H. Singer/Eve Swan-burg/Maggie & Walter
		Howard Glen, 1899/ Hazel M. Dean/ Maggie & Walter
	Millie A., 1878/died/ Jacob & Jennie	
	Cora Lula, 1879/ James Andrew **Campbell**/Jacob & Jennie	Ralph Lorenzo, 1897/?/Cora & Jim
		Donald M., 1898/?/ Cora & Jim
		Ivanilla R., 1902/?/ Cora & Jim
		George W. 1916/?/ Cora & Jim

Whitcomb Family	1st GENERATION Child, birth/Spouse/ Parents	2nd GENERATION Child, birth/Spouse/ Parents
Whitcomb, George Dexter, 1834/Leadora Bennett	George Bennett, 1860/Meda Ella Shepperd/George Dexter & Leadora	George Ernest, 1886/Hazel Gwinn/ Meda & George Bennett
		Walter Roland, 1888/died 1899/ Meda & George Bennett
		Arella, 1892/died 1899/Meda & George Bennett
		Leadora, 1893/ died 1899/Meda & George Bennett
	Henry, 1863/died 1864/George Dexter & Leadora	
	Carroll Sylvanus, 1865/Ada Bradley/ Laura S. Sellers/ George Dexter & Leadora	Bessie May, 1888/?/ Carroll & Ada
		Carroll C., 1890/?/ Carroll & Ada
		Orlena, 1981/?/ Carroll & Ada
		Wilbur Bradley, 1897/?/Carroll & Ada
		Dorothy, 1900/?/ Carroll & Ada

Whitcomb Family	1st GENERATION Child, birth/Spouse/ Parents	2nd GENERATION Child, birth/Spouse/ Parents
		Lambert, 1917/?/ Carroll & Laura
	William Card, 1868/?/George Dexter & Leadora	
	Leadora, 1871/?/ George Dexter & Leadora	
	Elizabeth Emily, 1873/?/George Dexter & Leadora	
	Virginia, 1877/?/ George Dexter & Leadora	

Chadwick Family	1st GENERATION Child, birth/Spouse/Parents	2nd GENERATION Child, birth/Spouse/Parents	3rd GENERATION Child, birth/Spouse/Parents	4th GENERATION Child, birth/Spouse/Parents
Chadwick, James 1839/ Mary Gregson	George, 1865/?/James & Mary			
	Alice Maude, 1871/Frank H. Shepperd/James & Mary			
	Alberta Louisa, 1880/William Giles **Clardy**/James & Mary	Edwin James, 1898/?/Alberta & William		
		Edith Rose, 1899/Edward Milton **Love**/Alberta & William	Milton Edward, 1918/Emily Glee **Wilson**/Edith & Edward	6 children
			Stanley J., 1920/?/Edith & Unknown	Michael, c. 1946 /?/Stanley & ?
				Stanley, c. 1946/?/Stanley & ?
			Marjorie Jean, 1926/Robert **Hillman**/Edith & Edward	Robert, c. 1948/?/Marjorie & Robert
				Linda, c. 1948/Pederson?/ Marjorie & Robert

Index

Z

Photo Credits

All photographs are from Layne Staral's Collection unless used by permission and noted here.

Homesteaders

Sarah and John Casey, 1865, news clipping, *Azusa Pomotropic*.

Azusa Valley Homesteaders Map, 1937, by permission of the Azusa Historical Museum.

The Oregon Whitcombs

Packers and hunters, c. 1900, news clipping, Sweet Home Genealogical Society.

1895 Linking Pioneer Genes

Glendora Christian Church, northeast corner of Wabash and Bennett Avenues, by permission of Bob Hillman.

J.W. De Shields Market, 1905-1910, by permission of the Glendora Historical Museum.

Ad for J.W. De Shields Grocery, 1908, *La Palma*, Citrus High School annual, by permission of the Glendora Historical Museum.

The Cullen Legacy

The photographs of Bill Cullen, and of his daughter Karen and her husband Dan Wilshire were taken by Layne Staral in 2007. The rest are used by permission of Karen Cullen and Dan Wilshire with the following exceptions:

May Engelhardt Cullen, the Christian missionary to Hawaii, c. 1902, by permission of the Glendora Historical Museum.

The Cullen women, c. 1890, by permission of the Glendora Historical Museum.

The Cullen family, c. 1895, by permission of the Glendora Historical Museum.

From the Civil War to Glendora

Jennie Porter Collins, by permission of Marquita Shepperd Barber.

Jacob Russell Shepperd, by permission of Marquita Shepperd Barber.

Civil War tree envelope, by permission of Marquita Shepperd Barber.

Ad for the New Restaurant, Glendora *Signal*, March 1888.

Shepperd, Kamphefner, and De Shields families, 1910, by permission of Marquita Shepperd Barber.

Frank and Addie Shepperd, c. 1921,
by permission of Marquita Shepperd Barber.

William Shepperd's home, Route 66, c. 1910,
by permission of Marquita Shepperd Barber.

The Clardy-Engelhardt Legacy

Most of the photographs in this chapter are in the Engelhardt family album, used courtesy of Bob Hillman. Layne Staral took the picture of Bob Hillman in 2009. The exceptions are the following pictures:

Wedding picture, Dr. August and Rosa Engelhardt, May 1887,
by permission of the Glendora Historical Museum.

Henry D. Engelhardt's home, c. 1885,
by permission of the Glendora Historical Museum.

Henry D. Engelhardt's family, c. 1885,
by permission of the Glendora Historical Museum.

Dr. August and Rosa Engelhardt with their three sons, c. 1907,
by permission of the Glendora Historical Museum.

Glendora's Water Dowser

William Russell Shepperd, by permission of Marquita Shepperd Barber.

Alice May Kammerdiener, by permission of Marquita Shepperd Barber.

Bill Shepperd's business card, by permission of Marquita Shepperd Barber.

Juanita Shepperd, girls basketball, Glendora, 1922,
by permission of Marquita Shepperd Barber.

Shepperd family on porch, by permission of Marquita Shepperd Barber.

Bathing picture, by permission of Marquita Shepperd Barber.

Bill Shepperd and probably Alice, by permission of
Marquita Shepperd Barber.

The Memoirs of Frances De Shields Metzger, Parts One and Two

Gladstone House, photo and permission by Dale Martin.

On the Cover

One copy of the cover photograph of the Settlers of the East San Gabriel Valley on Memorial Day 1950 is on display in the Azusa Historical Museum with a list of names along its bottom border. Unfortunately, the list does not separate the rows, so it's impossible to put the names to the faces. That said, I can identify the attendees in the first row because my family members are those seated on the ground. I'm including a left-to-right list of them below. The woman holding the baby in the center of the photo is Maggie De Shields, and the child is Yvonne De Shields, one of her great-granddaughters. I'm also sharing an alphabetized list of the other old-timers.

A second copy of the 1950 photograph is displayed in the Glendora Historical Society along with the 1927 picnic picture with a Union soldier in uniform in the center. GAR–Grand Army of the Republic is on his hat. There is no list of 1927 attendees, though my family is represented.

Most pioneer picnics were held at Azusa City Hall from 1922 until 1973. The venue provided both an auditorium where the group could hold a meeting, and a spacious area around it for picnicking and children's games. The 1950 photograph was taken there. Occasionally the picnic group gathered at Pioneer Park on Sierra Madre Avenue.

Seated front row, (l-r):

Jean De Shields Bacchilega,
  pregnant with son Danny
Frank Bacchilega
Glen De Shields with grandson
  Jimmy Duff on his lap
Billie De Shields
Bobby De Shields
Sharon De Shields
Jamie Ann Duff
Bob De Shields Sr. with
  Frankie Bacchilega in front of him
Bob De Shields Jr.
Virginia De Shields
Unidentified man
June De Shields Duff
Bill Jones
Bill Staral
Carl Metzger
Hazel De Shields

Other attendees:

Alverado, Mrs. Granville
Ayres, Clara
Barnes, Mrs. Leo
Beardsley, D.C.
Bently, Mrs.
Bently, Mr.
Briggs, Mrs. D.
Briggs, Dwight
Briggs, Raymond
Brown
Campbell, Collin Francis
Campbell, Mrs. Collen or Cullen
Cullen, Kathleen
Daniels, mother, Lee
Davis, Genn
Denny Marvin
Glover, Maria
Glover, Sarge
Granville
Haskell, Mrs.
Haskell, Mr.

Hawkins, Milo (maybe Dawkins)
Inman, Emma (De Shields)
Inman, Vivian (Miller)
Kelsaw, Mrs. (Rory)
Kurtz, Stella
Lee, Mr.
Lee, Mrs.
Lovelace, Walter
Mading
Marvin, Denny
Millar, Wm.
Millar, Mrs. Peter (Rogers)
Miller & Mrs. Wm (Spencer)
Moon, Mrs. Wm.
Moranes
Morden, Mrs. Eva
Morton, Mrs. Nora
Mowers, Mrs.
Munroe, Mrs.
Parkinson, Mr. Henry
Parkinson, Mrs. Colleen
Pelly, Mrs. John
Pettig, Mr. John
Preston, Minnie
Preston, Mrs. Jim
Ray, Mrs.
Remaley, Wm.
Richardson, Myrtle
Richardson, Charles
Richardson, Earl
Rogers, Henry
Rogers, Mr. Harry
Rory, Christine
Rottenbein, Mrs.
Runy, Ward
Rury, Wm.
Sheldon
Sheldon
Smith
Smith, Mr. Edgar
Smith, Mrs. Edgar
Snavely
Spencer, Mr. Donell
Tarkinson
Thompson, Mr. Ed
Wells, Mrs.
White, Millie
Williams, Fred
Williams, Edwin
Zarrell

Acknowledgments

This book is an act of love. I started researching and writing articles on my family history in 2006, so it's taken almost twenty years to complete. I owe Ida and the late Joe Fracasse and their daughter Lynn Nobbs a huge debt of gratitude for publishing my articles. Assembling so much information and then adding family pictures to the stories was a huge undertaking, but now that the information is assembled, I hope my family and many other families share in the joys of the earliest Azusa Valley pioneers.

Many of the wonderful people who helped me research my family are gone, and I may forget to mention someone important to this book. My list of helpers will be incomplete, but here it is.

Anna Lafferty has turned my words into a gorgeous book. I can't thank her enough for making the process fun. Her cover design caught the spirit of the pioneers, and her enthusiasm for the stories shows on every page. Anna's friend, Susan Gulbransen, brought Anna and me together for this project. Susan and her husband Gary have welcomed me annually into their home for over thirty years while I've attended the Santa Barbara Writers Conference, and Susan has been an inspiration, her husband a source of tech support.

My friend Linda Colley is a fine critic. She found many mistakes and enjoyed most the sentences that prompted unintentional laughs. For example, I wrote that my great-great-grandmother, who was wheelchair-bound in Glendora in 1910, often visited her daughter in Santa Monica. Linda hoped she found a better means of transportation. My extraordinary proofreader, Marsha Barr, fine-tuned corrections I didn't know I needed, and Erin Graffy is proving to be a supportive and informative publisher.

My niece Qiana Tarlow and nephew Shaun Staral prompted me to put my articles together in a book. Their enthusiasm has helped me focus on a goal and the future. My friends from elementary school, Trisha Melcher and Bonny Hidas, are supporting and encouraging me through life. And through his personal lens, Bob Keys shared all forms of beauty and excellence with me. I still feel the warmth of his light.

My family members:

The Starals and Tarlows in Santa Clarita; the Johnsons in Montrose; the De Shields in Huntington Beach; the Bacchilegas in Carpinteria; Karen Cullen and Dan Wilshire in Glendora; Lisa and David Grigolla in Montclair; Darell and Dorothy Clark in Arizona.

In memoriam: Marquita Barber, Reta De Shields Parton, Jean and Frank Bacchilega.

The Glendora Historical Society:

Karen Cullen, Dan Wilshire, Carol Treacy, Scott Rubel, Ryan Price, Karen Garcia, Ida Fracasse, Lynn Nobbs, Edwin Anderson, Steve Flowers, Jeffrie Hall, Jesse Tomory, and more.

In memoriam: John Lundstrom, Joe Fracasse, Zella Cramer, Georgia Hawthorne, Margaret House, Kay Waters, De De Tomory, Skeeter Kobzeff, Norma Rowley, Lambert Whitcomb, and Bill Cullen.

Azusa Historical Society and Library:

Jeffrey Cornejo, Dale and Evelyn Martin, Suzanne Avila.

In memoriam: Jennie Avila. Karen Shomber found many originals in the Azusa files for me, including Maggie De Shields' handwritten secretary notes for the pioneer picnic records, a photo of the Taggart women, and John Casey's deed that made him the first filer for land in the Azusa Valley under American control.

Oregon Correspondents:

Sharon Leader, Sweet Home Genealogical Society; Shawna Gandy, archivist, Oregon Historical Society in Portland; Pat Dunn, Lebanon Genealogical Society.

Other Listeners and Supporters:

Fred Peritore, Daniel Bartosz, Cathy Black, Linda Pederson, Richard Benda, Natalie Gray, Jean Rowe, Sally Abood, Fred Nahra, Anne Edkins, Nancy Boyarsky, Ray Tyndall, Al Clark, Ralph Kuncl, Elizabeth Pomeroy, Oliver Beckwith, and more.

In memoriam: Pete Hidas and Bob Hillman.

About the Author

Layne D. Staral is a sixth generation Californian. Her ancestors homesteaded the Azusa Valley with other settlers in the 1850s and eventually participated in the building of the towns of Azusa and Glendora. Before she was twenty, she attended the annual Pioneer Picnics with her family, and since she retired from teaching in 2005, Layne has been a volunteer in the Glendora and Azusa Historical Museums. She's written articles for the *Glendoran* magazine on the early history of the valley, and she's also been responsible for converting the reel-to-reel oral history tapes to a digital format. In 2009, she provided both museums with an accessible typed manuscript of the water commissioners' proceedings from 1871 to 1888 when the old ledger was found in storage. She has a Master's in English from Cal State University, Los Angeles, and an MFA in Writing from Vermont College. She is also a member of First Century Families.

About the Book Designer

Anna Lafferty of Lafferty Design Plus, is an award-winning graphic designer who creates book layouts and produces them for authors and small publishers. She has a B.A. from UCLA, an MAEd from the University of Hartford, and an MFA from Syracuse University. Anna developed classes in graphics, publication, and book design as a tenured professor at Tunxis Community College, near Hartford, Connecticut, and at Sacred Heart University, in Fairfield, CT. She received a Faculty Mellon Fellowship in Graphic Design at Yale University. Returning to her home town of Santa Barbara, California, she developed a graphic design program for UCSB Extension and taught at the School of Media Arts at Santa Barbara City College for over twenty years. She was on the founding Board of the American Institute of Graphic Arts, Santa Barbara, and has developed specialty online zoom classes in InDesign for small professional groups. Anna has been in the forefront of graphic design during its changing technologies. It's been an exciting ride and she remains respected for her knowledge and experience.

Made in the USA
Las Vegas, NV
03 March 2025

19023093R00105